I FLEW
WITH
HELL'S ANGELS

Thirty-six Combat Missions
in a
B-17 "Flying Fortress"
1944-1945

By Bill Albertson
from the Memoirs of
2nd Lt. Edward Albertson
303rd Bombardment Group (H)
359th Bomb Squadron, Eighth Air Force

EAGLE EDITIONS
2007

EAGLE EDITIONS
AN IMPRINT OF HERITAGE BOOKS, INC.

Books, CDs, and more—Worldwide

For our listing of thousands of titles see our website
at
www.HeritageBooks.com

Published 2007 by
HERITAGE BOOKS, INC.
Publishing Division
65 East Main Street
Westminster, Maryland 21157-5026

International Standard Book Number: 978-0-7884-3506-5

But Thou, O Lord, be gracious
to me, and raise me up,
That I may repay them.
By this I know that Thou art
pleased with me,
Because my enemy does not
shout in triumph over me.

Psalms 41:10, 11

Greater love has no one than this,
that one lay down his life for his
friends.

John 15: 13

CONTENTS

FOREWORD

As a boy growing up on the southern shores of the Chesapeake Bay, I remember wondering why my dad's knuckles would bleed on cold, snowy days. Curious, I asked my father how he hurt his hands. "Oh, that's nothing son, it's just something that happened during the war." At that time the answer satisfied me, but as I grew older, and after asking him repeatedly, my father told me his knuckles became that way as a result of frostbite he received as a navigator aboard B-17 bombers flying out of England during World War II. I started to ask more questions and paid close attention to his accounts of the missions he flew (thirty-six in all) over Germany, where an airman's fate depended not only on his training and the training of his fellow crewmembers but also on the luck of the draw; where every mission could be his last.

I would sit and watch the movie "Twelve O'Clock High" and the television series of the same name with my father, paying close attention when actual air combat scenes taken from WWII archives would appear. He would say, "That's one of our ships," or "that's a true picture," meaning it was a plane from his squadron, part of the famous "Hell's Angels" Bomb Group.

Later, I don't know why, but I found myself jotting down the names of crewmembers, the places they bombed and the names of some of the ships he flew aboard. At some point after my father's death in 1995, I decided to collect his war stories in book form.

I began by reading books about the Eighth Air Force and came across a website of the 303rd Bomb Group (H) Association, better known as "Hell's Angels." There I found the names of crew members my father flew with as well as the dates of the bombing missions. At the National Archives in College Park, Maryland, I discovered a wealth of detailed information: not only names and dates but actual pilots' accounts and original reports of bombing raids; photographs, including air combat shots; tonnage of bombs dropped; rounds fired; enemy aircraft encountered; casualties; even weather reports. With this new information, and with the permission of the National Archives and the 303rd Bomb Group (H)

Association, Inc., I was able to document the stories I remembered as a boy.

This book is written for all the children (including my daughter), grandchildren, and future generations; the descendants of those brave men who flew, died and survived. I hope these future generations will never forget what it took and what a price these men paid to secure the freedoms we have to this day.

The pictures in this book are not only of B-17 bombers and not just of Hell's Angels. The men who flew in these and other bombers and fighters, and who fought in the skies over Europe, did so by the thousands. Pictures from other groups and in other planes represent what every man went through as all of them had similar, frightening experiences.

I relate these stories in the first person as I remember my father telling them to me, speaking in his frank, straightforward style.

I glance at a photograph of my father, 2nd Lieutenant Edward Albertson: a few months out of high school, eighteen years old, no more than a kid. I try to imagine what it was like for him and the boys he flew with; to be in his shoes as his B-17 lifted off a runway in England on one of those famous bombing missions.

As you look at the pictures, look closely and keenly. Envision what these boys were thinking, what they were feeling. As you do this, imagine some of them not coming home as indeed, some of them were killed and never made it back. Now, as you turn these pages, you will always think of them differently, as though frozen in time.

I cannot begin to convey what it was like to actually fly with Hell's Angels, but through my father's remembrances, collected in this volume, perhaps others will gain a sense of that time and place in history; and an appreciation for the brave men who flew those missions which were to become the glory of their youth.

ACKNOWLEDGMENTS

I want to thank Jack Nelson for all his help and guidance in the writing of this book. His time, knowledge and patience with a novice author will always be appreciated. And especially to Julia Shubert, who after reading the first and only three pages persuaded me to continue. Because of her encouragement, writing this book was a pleasure.

INTRODUCTION

They called our outfit the "Hell's Angels." Officially, we were the 303rd Bombardment Group (H), of the Eighth Air Force, United States Army Air Corps. Our bombardment group consisted of four bomber squadrons: the 358th, 359th, 360th and the 427th. I flew with the 359th Squadron. We flew out of England from 1942 thru 1945. And we flew the greatest planes ever manufactured: the nearly indestructible B-17, known as "The Flying Fortress."

Between 1935 and 1945 there were 12,731 B-17s built. Of these, 4,750 were lost in aerial combat. My Group alone (the 303rd) lost 210 Flying Fortresses, taking with them 841 of the bravest men war has known. Another 747 airmen managed to escape their doomed bombers by way of parachutes. Most were captured by the Germans and became prisoners of war. Of the planes that went down from my group, sixty-five were shot down by enemy aircraft. Nearly as many, fifty-two, were brought down by flak. Also, there were twenty-three B-17s that had to ditch in the sea, thirteen crash-landed and six planes were lost to mid-air collisions.

As the air battle raged in the skies over Germany, thousands of young men—boys really—faced horrifying death on nearly a daily basis. Bombing raids to Dresden, Bremen, Wilhelmshaven, Stuttgart, Merseburg, Berlin and dozens of other German cities took a staggering toll of American youth.

A fellow had to complete twenty-five missions—later upped to thirty, then thirty-five—before his tour was over and he could return stateside. The only hitch lay in the fact that in 1943 the average flyboy became a casualty by his fifteenth mission.

I was just an average guy who was lucky to get through it, serving with other average guys from all over the United States, a lot of them, not so lucky.

2nd Lieutenant Edward Albertson
303rd Bomb Group, 359th Bomb Squadron, Eighth Air Force

PART ONE

THE BEGINNING

It was November 20, Thanksgiving Day 1942, and the annual rivalry between the two high school football teams, Granby and Wilson, was an hour away.

As we sat on the cold, wooden benches in the darkened, damp locker rooms, we wondered what the outcome would be in three hours' time. Win or lose, each combatant knew it would be a hard-fought contest.

The whistle blew, and the kicker booted a perfect end-over-end. The boys started the opening sprint, anxious to give the first blow. The smell of wet grass and dry chalk, which would grow sacred over the years, suddenly yielded to hard swift pain as the enemy slammed into me, his steel-tipped cleats raking across my calf, and ripping off the week-old scabs from my elbows.

"Bamm!" Boy, that fellow really unloaded on me that time. Landing on the half-frozen turf felt like hitting concrete pavement. Every time I hit or was hit, each bone in my body seemed to give way. Back and forth the contest went, banging heads, knocking the enemy back, taking hits and bouncing back up, ready to fight again. Over and over, a score for us, one for them, back and forth until the final whistle sounded and the game was over.

It was time to shake hands and congratulate the foe. For the seniors on both squads came the realization that after spring graduation these former opponents would be on the same team fighting in one capacity or another the real enemy: the Nazis and the Japs.

Once June arrived I had only three things to do: graduate, celebrate my eighteenth birthday and sign up for the Army Air Corps. Then it would be on to basic training.

I thought it wouldn't be too bad, surely not any worse than summer football practice and besides, I was still in pretty good shape. I didn't believe I would have to worry much. Just follow instructions, do what I'm told, do it right, do it quickly, and with a lot of hustle, just like my father told me. That same discipline and attitude had gotten him through basic before he left for France and "The war to end all wars" in 1918.

The bus pulled up to camp at 1:15 A.M. and some sergeant yelled "OK you babies, move your asses! What do you think this is, some damn football training camp?" I started to realize right then that maybe I could have been wrong about some of my assumptions.

It didn't take too long to hustle through to get our gear and personal items, be assigned barracks and bunk and to be introduced to our new drill sergeant. *Now I know I'm in the Army Air Corps! This is it; I'm here to become a flyboy. After flight training I'm off to kill Krauts or Japs, doesn't matter, either one is OK with me. I'm ready for the real game to begin.*

Bamm bamm bamm bamm! "Up, you morons, let's go! Let's move it," a voice from the darkness bellowed.

Who the hell is that? I thought. *What time is it?* It was 4 A.M.!

"Get in to your P.T. gear, ladies; it's time to get into physical condition, no more lying around, move it!" I was really beginning to dislike the guy behind this voice.

Jumping jacks, push-ups, knee bends, log rolls (I always hated log rolls). More push-ups, running in place. *This isn't so bad,* I thought; *not as bad as coach back home. A few more minutes of this and maybe we can have some breakfast.*

"All right, ladies, fall in, time to jog a few miles!" the drill sergeant shouted.

Five miles and nearly fifty minutes later and totally out of breath, then it was time to exercise even more: more push-ups and sit-ups and more of those damned log rolls!

Finally, chow and coffee and rest for a while. Nope, wrong again, more physical training. *Damn.*

The first day of training is now over. Thank God. Tomorrow I hope will be better. I don't believe I will have any trouble getting to sleep tonight.

Bamm Bamm Bamm! 4 A.M.

Torture, this was torture, waddling around in the steamy grass over the driest dirt I had ever inhaled. Dirt under my fingernails, in my nostrils, eyes burning of salt from my own sweat. *God dammit*

Sergeant, why do I need this to fly? I thought. Over and over and over the same old stuff, week after week. Each time I thought all this training was getting easier, the drill sergeant increased our exercises and running. Turns out high school football did help, but not as much as I thought.

After three weeks I found I didn't get as tired. I was in excellent shape. Twenty times better shape than back home. While lying awake in my bunk waiting for the sergeant to beat the trashcan to wake us, I thought how fun it would be to start flying, but right at that moment all I wanted was a good breakfast with lots of hot coffee.

All of us looked forward to mealtime. But what kind of breakfast was this? Corned beef hash slop and the worst tasting eggs I ever swallowed. These damn things taste like powder; actually more like grit or silt. This stuff is such a contrast to what we ate at home. Growing up on the beach was fun but I worked hard to help my family eat. During the Depression the family moved from the inner city neighborhood of Larchmont, Virginia, to the lower shores of the Chesapeake Bay to a place called Ocean View.

There we could fish, crab, tong for oysters and dig for clams. We boys worked hard to help the family. I know this may sound crazy to most but I actually got tired of eating seafood. Now what I wouldn't give for some Ocean View spot (that small tender, tasty fish) or flounder or blue crabs and some of that steamy, warm, clam chowder. Back then we had no money, few clothes and little else, but we did eat well. When others were lucky enough to eat chicken backs and necks we ate our choice of highly prized seafood and baked goods my mother made. Often my mother would help out others by baking them cakes, pies and fried bread. After finishing what she was making for the neighbors, my brothers and sister would lay claim to the rest. Her rolls were mouth-watering and her fried bread…my brother Douglas and I fought over. *Boy, I could go for some of those meals right now.*

"Attention!"

Now what? I thought.

"All right boys, enough of stuffing your bellies, it's time to take a little walk. Be ready in ten minutes with full packs. Dismissed!"

Eight miles and a lot of cuss words later we finished. I thought, *Now I'm ready for anything. I am sure ready to get the hell out of here.*

On to flight school. *This will be fun. I can't wait to get on with it.* All of my buddies were ready to do their duty. *Let's get moving and whip some Krauts.*

"Albertson! Report to HQ. The lieutenant wants to see you," the sergeant ordered.

"Sir. Yes, sir." I answered.

Twenty minutes later I was told I was going to be a navigator, not a pilot. "Excuse me Lieutenant; I want to be a pilot."

"You'll be a navigator or you'll be working in the mess hall for the rest of the war. Now get your butt over to building six and report in," the lieutenant barked back.

"Yes, sir." What else could I say? Damn, what luck. But I would be flying just as high and at least I'd be able to shoot back with a fifty-caliber machine gun, since the navigator was positioned up front in the nose. The pilot and co-pilot were the only ones of the ten crew members without any weapons. Now that I think about it, I'd rather be able to fire back.

I trained at Ellington Field in Texas for nine weeks. After that it was on to Coral Gables, Florida for ten weeks of advanced training.

Nineteen weeks of training and now I'm ready—I think, I hope. We have flown many training flights and we looked good. Tomorrow we will get our assignment to a bomber group.

Two nights earlier we had been flying at 20,000 feet at 200 miles per hour. I took a reading and looked below to confirm we were over Miami. Twenty minutes later the pilot asked for another reading so we could make our turn and head south. When I checked my instruments I could not believe what I was seeing. We were at the same spot we had been twenty minutes earlier. I told the pilot to make a 180-degree turn and I would check again. What I found was that we were flying into a 200-mile-per-hour headwind! *That doesn't happen often; I hope the winds over Europe are not as strong. I hear the enemy flak is pretty accurate and we will need all the air speed we can get.*

We were gathered together the next morning after chow, waiting for our orders when our CO entered and said, "Gentlemen. You have a choice of either the 91st Bomb Group or the 303rd Bomb Group. You choose, boys, you deserve it."

At once a unanimous yell went out. "The 303rd!" This was the group that Clark Gable flew for: you know, Rhett Butler, "Gone With the Wind;" "The King" of the movies! Gable flew five missions for the Air Force, some for Hell's Angels in the 359th Squadron in 1943 as a gunner before he was sent back to the states. Moviemakers wanted him to do recruiting films for the Army Air Corps but he refused unless he was actually in the service fighting as the rest of the boys were. I'm sure he would have flown more if he were not pulled off future missions for fear the Germans would go after his plane. If he had been shot down and killed or captured I'm sure the Germans would have had a field day with the propaganda, not to mention the loss of morale to us.

Man, this is going to be better than I could have wished for. Wait until my girl back home hears about this. This is great. Flying with the famous Hell's Angels! I never could have imagined.

I had a week's leave before we were to ship out. Once at home I could get everything squared away. I wondered how I would find everyone.

My girl met me at the bus station. Boy, what a sight to see! Betty June; all of her friends called her Blue Jay because of her sparkling blue eyes.

I remember the first day I saw her. I was hanging out at the old bowling alley near home when I saw this blonde-haired, blue-eyed beauty walk in. I fell head over heels right then. In that instant, I knew she was the one for me. We dated all through high school even though her mother didn't care much for me. I wasn't good enough I suppose. You know, not from the right neighborhood, always getting into fights and trouble at school. To tell the truth, I didn't much care for her mother either. Betty June and I were going to marry and her mother couldn't do a thing about it. The only thing that could stop us was if I was killed in the war. And I didn't plan on that happening. As we took a cab from the bus station back to my parents' house I started thinking of some of my father's military experiences.

My father was on the battlefields of France in 1918 and had a hell of a time at the Battle of Belleau Wood. Maybe, since I'd be shipping out soon, he would give me the straight scoop, you know, about what to expect in combat and everything. I remembered speaking with a neighbor, "Old Man" Nugent, about one of my father's WWI experiences. He told me the story about a certain battle in which my father captured this German officer. It went like this:

It seems he was ordered to capture a German officer, for intelligence purposes I suppose. Anyway, he went out on a night patrol with six or seven other guys. The squad was ambushed and everyone was killed except my father. When he stumbled back into camp alone, the CO yelled, "God dammit Albertson, I told you to bring back a prisoner, now don't come back here again without a God dammed German officer, understand!"

Sometime around dawn he returned, all bloody and tattered. He shoved this German to the ground at the CO's feet and said: "Here's your God dammed prisoner sir," turned round on his heels and walked off. When the sun was well up later that morning, as "Old Man" Nugent related, everyone in camp discovered what had transpired the night before. At nearly the exact spot where his buddies had been massacred hours before, at least twelve dead Germans were laid out where they fell and a machine gun nest had been destroyed. Some had been shot at point-blank range, some knifed. My father never talked much about it.

It was nice seeing everyone, spending a few days with my girl and just taking it easy. We rested from the classes, chores and exercises all of us back at training went through every day.

When it came time for me to leave, my mother didn't say much, only to take care and come back home. My father shook my hand and said to do my best. He was a man of few words. I knew he was very fond of an old record he used to listen to on the phonograph that gave me pause when I heard it. When I asked him why he liked it so much he said this was the song that his father sang to him when he went off to fight in World War I.

I was ready to leave and head off to do my part in this war, but leaving Blue Jay was tough. I believed we would be married when I returned but there was always the chance I would not get back; and the thought of my girl with another man drove me nuts. I had been in more fights in school over her than I care to remember.

When Betty June and I said our goodbyes I could tell the heartbreak and sorrow for her was at times overwhelming. I assured her that I would be careful and would not do anything stupid and that I would return. Then I kissed her and told her, reassured her, I would come back.

"Ed," she said, "you are not invincible, for God's sake take care of yourself."

"I will, honey," I replied, "I promise." I always thought being wounded or killed was what happened to the other guys, not me. The taxi ride to the bus depot was somber but I felt that once I was aboard a troop ship and on my way to England I would be OK.

When I arrived in New York City after an all-night bus trip I had a couple of hours to kill. I walked for a while before ducking into a bar for some coffee. There I heard that Irish song that my father liked so much. My thoughts went back to my father smoking a cigar and reading one of his books while the phonograph played, "Oh Danny Boy, the pipes, the pipes are calling, from glen to glen and down the mountain side..." I never knew why he enjoyed that tune so much until then. I slowly finished my coffee and then headed to my departure point.

Once my gear was loaded aboard ship I realized, *This is it.* I couldn't wait to get into the thick of things. We departed on November 1, 1944.

After three days at sea I thought, this is a bunch of mess. So many men were cramped in that old tub. I was sharing a bunk with two other guys rotating on eight-hour shifts. The smell of cigarette smoke combined with diesel fuel and puke made us all ready to punch anyone who looked at us wrong and many a fight broke out.

Gambling was the only thing that made the trip worthwhile. One game of craps was being played that drew a lot of attention and that was the one where Sergeant Burkett was making an unbelievable run. I was watching him win roll after roll until he said, "Let it ride, boys. This will be my last play."

He must have been insane! He was letting nearly $18,000 in winnings ride on a last roll! He was rich! Money was changing hands on side bets like crazy including twenty bucks from me to see him lose. I thought, *There is no way this guy can roll another winner*, especially since he had won fifteen in a row. I knew his chances were nil. I was trying to borrow money from some buddies to bet but could not get any takers. "Come on fellows, ante up, there is no possible way Burkett can do this again."

The tension was so high you couldn't hear yourself think. Then Burkett rolled. I didn't see what he rolled but from the reaction of others I knew the son of a gun won! *Damn, I thought! There goes another twenty. That lucky bastard just walked away with thousands!* I remembered thinking he'd better be careful with all that cash. Later that day I heard Burkett lost every bit of his winnings in another game. I knew his luck would run out sooner or later.

We would soon be in England and I couldn't wait. *I'm ready to get back to work flying and to do my part.* By that time my older brother Douglas had made half a dozen or so landings in the Pacific with the First Marine Division.

I remember when the Japs attacked Pearl Harbor; Doug was talking to Father about joining up. My father strongly suggested that he join the Navy and try to stay away from the heaviest fighting. I was surprised to hear Doug agree. He said at that time he would do what our father suggested. A few days later Doug asked to talk to Dad.

"I've decided to go against your advice, Dad."

"What are you talking about son?" our father asked.

"I've joined the Marines. I want to take it to those bastards for what they did to us," my brother said. "You went with your choice in WWI and I'm going to do the same."

I was watching my father, trying to guess what he would say. To my surprise all I saw was a smile of approval and the words, "OK son, whatever you want."

My brother was smaller than me, but a tough boy. I wanted to be a flyboy and well, that's what I was doing. Nothing has more freedom to me than being in a plane in wide-open spaces—nothing.

A few days after my father's conversation with my brother I told him of my decision to join the Army Air Corps.

He turned his attention to me and then simply got out of his chair, flicked his cigar ashes and headed to his bedroom. A moment later he returned, unfolding a letter.

"This letter is dated September 14, 1925, from a man I admired above many others. It reads:

Dear Sir,
Thank you very much for your letter of September 6th.

Feeling as I do that this is the most vital and important problem before the Nation today, it is indeed a pleasure to receive an expression of this nature, and truly encouraging in that it is representative, I believe of what America feels on this subject.

Yours very truly,
Wm. Mitchell
Colonel, A.S.

"Son, Colonel Billy Mitchell was considered by many as the father of the modern Air Service. This is the same Billy Mitchell who predicted that the Japanese would bomb Pearl Harbor on a Sunday morning. I wrote him because I wanted him to know many of us veterans supported him, and to hell with the politicians.

"He was court-martialed in late 1925 and died on February 1, 1936, only a few years after you were born. Here's why:

"He was a man, a real man. He stood up and defied his superiors criticizing them for allowing the Japanese and some of the European countries to move forward with their air services while doing nothing about our own country's air defenses. He told the truth when others in the Army, Navy and in Congress refused to open their eyes and their mouths, too damn scared of losing their positions and their importance.

"Thank goodness we now have leaders that realize Mitchell's wisdom and are taking action to make our Air Service the most powerful in the world.

"When you complete your training, take what you learn and put it to good use. Stand up for our beliefs and fight for our freedoms and the freedom of others. This, in part, I believe, is the meaning of a true American.

"Now you know what I think of you joining the Air Corps."

As my father slowly folded his letter, putting it carefully back in its envelope, I knew all I needed to know and what I had to do.

ENGLAND

Our arrival to England was slow in coming but on November 15, 1944, we finally made it. My base was to be in Molesworth, the home of the famed "Hell's Angels" of the 303rd Bomb Group.

It was a lot colder there than I thought it would be. The snow was nearly knee deep, and getting around was slow. But I thought after a few days I would get used to it and find my way around.

I was assigned to the crew of 2nd Lt. Alfred Holmes, a tall lanky fellow from El Paso, Texas. His friends called him Tex.

Some of the squadrons had steel Nissen huts but most of the barracks, including mine, were low, long, wooden, cold-looking buildings set about a foot off the ground.

The officers' barracks were divided into four-man rooms. As I followed Tex to our assigned spaces the staff sergeant said, "These two are for you; take your pick. The former residents were killed last week over Gelsenkirchen."

In the room stood a small potbellied stove. We were told our ration of coal had to last the week. Looking at some of the other rooms, I noticed six or seven blankets per bed. I thought to myself, this is going to be a cold one. Out back there was a latrine and a bomb shelter dug out with a pile of dirt about five or six feet high surrounding it.

Tex asked the staff sergeant, "How many times has this bomb shelter been used?" But I don't believe he was really looking for an answer.

West of our location, the 360th Squadron was lodged. Just south was the main east-west runway. All I really wanted now was to get settled and get some hot food; even if I had to eat some of that slop, at least it would be warm.

Later that day we were told to be ready for some practice runs early the next morning. That night I found out the hard way, why the men were using so many blankets.

I will never forget that first night in England. The cold was everywhere. Everything was covered with snow and inside the hut frost was all over everything: our cups, razors, everything. The three blankets assigned to me were just not going to make it. We had used half a week's worth of coal that first night! Luckily we were awakened at about 0430 and told to be ready to fly by 0730. Breakfast at 0515 to 0600, briefing at 0615.

The snow was too deep to walk side by side. I followed Tex down a narrow shoveled path to the mess hall, which was about fifty yards away but seemed more like fifty miles in the icy weather. We laced our fur-lined flight jackets up to the neck and pulled our hoods down over our faces to buck the stinging cold. We wasted no time stamping the snow off our boots to get inside, quickly forming a line by the stoves. There were already a lot of boys who had staked out their places by the stoves, eating silently. I noticed an unusual quiet. I learned later that a few days before that, black market punks from Liverpool had stolen most of the eggs and bacon so we were stuck eating powdered eggs and Spam. There were only two cooks to feed nearly a hundred fliers. I settled for coffee, toast and a smoke that first morning.

After a week's worth of practice flying and learning the ropes with our new crews, everyone was tired of practicing and ready to get on with the fighting. Before breakfast was over that day we were told to stand down. The weather was too bad to attempt taking off so we headed back to our barracks with nothing to do but wait.

This is a picture of our training crew in June 1944, before heading to England. Harry Jenkins, (bottom left) is the pilot. I'm at the bottom right. Photo courtesy of the 303rd Bomb Group Association and the National Archives.

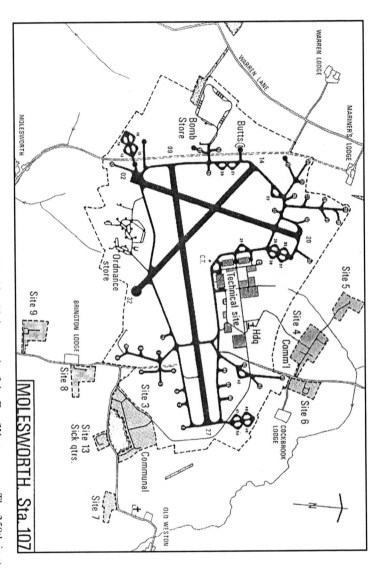

This is our base at Molesworth. The 359th is located at Site #6, just north of the East/West runway. The 358th is at Site #8 and the 360th at Site #5. The 427th is located next to the Technical Site. Courtesy of the National Archives.

PART TWO

NOVEMBER 26, 1944

Mission #1

Destination: Altenbeken

Target: Railroad Viaduct

By this time I had two blankets under me and nine over me, and was still cold as hell.

At 2 A.M. a bright flashlight shone in my eyes. An orderly awakened me. At last, I was glad to be on the list of fliers scheduled for that day's mission.

"Tex, hit the deck!" I yelled, and pulled my clothes from between the blankets where I kept them warm.

Tex struggled out of his cot cussing. I delighted in hearing the descriptive and quite apt words he used when commenting on dear old England. Such verbal enthusiasm as that could only come from one type of American, a Texan!

Here we go again, on that damned walk to the mess hall. This time I had my fill of powdered eggs and Spam plus many cups of my beloved coffee.

Heading over to the equipment room to put on my flying gear, I noticed on either side of the quarter-mile apron the line of B-17s. The ground crews were checking the engines and other parts of the planes for a final time before takeoff. Up and down the apron, the snowplows were at work just as I had seen for the past few days, only this time I was going up and heading off on a raid.

We entered the briefing room to gather all the necessary information concerning the upcoming mission, and also to get the candy and food rations, escape kits, and necessary supplies for the run.

As soon as I entered the room I proceeded to the rear. Lighting up a cigarette, I sat down on the last bench. The briefing officer soon arrived, wearing a seriousness I had not seen before. The officer spread out his information sheets on the lecture stand and switched on the lights over the wall map, covered still by the large, roll-away black shade.

The commanding officer slowly took a cigarette out of his pocket. Straightening his notes several times, he awaited the assembled crew's complete attention.

"Your target today, gentlemen, is a railroad viaduct at Altenbeken and a railroad marshalling yard at Osnabruck, Germany," he began. With an air of authority he continued, "Your bombs will be 1,000-pounders and you will assemble over Harrington at 0500." Bombing altitudes will be between 18,000 and 23,000 feet with fifty-eight crews dispatched. Length of mission: six hours, twenty-five minutes."

With that we were out and on our way.

Our entire crew hopped into a jeep and made our way to our ship, serial number 44-8038. No name had been given this ship yet but we all were coming up with ideas.

Tex was the pilot, Harold Fravel the co-pilot. Tom Donovan was the bombardier. Tom, from Boston, seemed to really know his stuff, and Tex and Harold were also first rate. As navigator, I felt lucky to be part of this crew. Sprague, our engineer and top turret gunner; Prehatny, our radio operator and gunner; Vowels, our ball turret gunner; Bartkowski, the tail gunner; and Johnson, our waist gunner made up the rest of the crew. These guys would protect us against the enemy fighters on the bomb run. Now we were going to see just how well we were trained.

We pulled our equipment off the jeep and headed for the tent where we joined up with the ground crew until engine time. We stepped into the tent and gathered around the potbellied stove as we discussed the mission. Time seemed to drag on and on. We were all anxious to get going. Tex spent a few more minutes going over what he expected of each of us then wished us all good luck.

Talk went on about our hometowns, our families and our girls for about an hour or so until the time came to start our engines. I grabbed the door under the nose and with a jump and pull, threw my legs up into the plane. We took our positions in the ship, installed our fifty-calibers and began checking our equipment. Tex asked each man to sound off once we were all in our proper positions. "Navigator checking in," I replied.

The only thing missing is the red string stretched across the wall map pointing out our mission for the day. Photo courtesy of the National Archives.

359th Bomb Squadron, Mission: Altenbeken, 11/26/44, lead crew. Photo courtesy of the National Archives and the 303rd Bomb Group Association.

Then I adjusted my lamp and seat and started spreading out my maps and setting my courses. I noticed my stomach churning and my hands trembling. *This is it*, I thought, as I looked over at Donovan, who was breathing hard and wiping his lips.

Twenty minutes later we were taxiing to the strip and falling into position in a long procession of B-17s in the squadron.

This time it was for keeps. As Tex started increasing power, I began to think of home. Of Betty June, of my father and mother, my little sister and older brother and what they were doing. Then I remembered my brother Doug and a letter my father mailed to him last May explaining why he shouldn't worry too much about all the crap going on back home. How some people felt towards our men in service, more especially towards the men who had actually been fighting. The gist of it now as best I can remember is how fighting men band together and form a kinship that no other humans can or will ever identify with.

"Here we go, boys," Tex called out. The plane started vibrating and lurching forward. The headwinds were good but it still felt like we were moving awful slow, and this time with six thousand pounds of bombs!

No one said a word but I knew they must be thinking the same thing I was; anticipating what was to come, wondering, *would I make it, would I be killed, taken prisoner?* A thousand questions came to me all at once. Too many to answer. Slowly we climbed to nine thousand feet and assembled over our designated radio beacon with the squadron and headed for the English coast.

After arriving on schedule at our departure point I notified Tex and our squadron took its position in the group as we started over the Channel.

"OK boys, check your guns," Tex commanded. A moment later each of us shot off a few rounds.

Soon all settled down. We began preparing mentally and emotionally to do what we had been trained to do. I made another check of the wind speed and double-checked our ground and true air speed. All was well and only then did I look out the Plexiglas bubble up front and notice the beautiful blue sky and floating clouds below us. What a sight! True heaven! Nothing but beautiful, serene, wide-open spaces, interrupted only by the sound and sight of our B-17s.

These are planes from the 381st Bomb Group assembling over England on their way to bomb Germany. The air base is at the lower right. Photo courtesy of the National Archives.

This Me 109 was shot down by one of our P-47 fighters. Nice shot, boys. Photo courtesy of the National Archives.

Osnabruck was a town in northwest Germany. We were still a couple of hours from our drop point by my pilotage when the low rumble of engines was interrupted by the high, loud shout of, "Enemy fighters coming in at 2 o'clock!"

I swung my fifty-cal around to see two enemy Me 109 fighters closing fast, only to turn and break low, exposing their underbellies for a brief second or two.

"They're coming around again," shouted the tail gunner to the left waist. I turned in time to aim and pull the trigger. With the airplane bouncing up and down I knew I would only have an instant to score. As this Jerry pulled up beside us, I thought I was giving him hell until Donovan punched me in the back of my shoulder.

"What the hell was that for?" I yelled in excitement. I broke my concentration from Jerry and jerked a look to Donovan.

He was grinning and motioning with his arm to look down at my gun. Snatching away my oxygen mask, again I yelled, "What the hell are you doing, Donovan?"

Donovan pointed again to look down at my gun.

Glancing down and turning to the side, I then noticed my safety was on! *Jesus Christ,* I thought, *Jerry is probably laughing at me, thinking I'm an idiot.* By that time however, he was long gone. I was breathing harder than if I had just finished a four-mile run back at basic.

Being on the bomb run and close to our drop point, I knew we could not take any evasive action. Tex radioed Donovan that we were approximately three minutes until bombs away and to make sure he dropped our bombs as soon as the lead ship did. The Kraut fighters were now concentrating on the 427th Squadron leader's plane piloted by Captain Healy. Everything was happening at once. Dogfights were everywhere. Our P-51s were shooting down German Me 210s and Me 109s.

Then an explosion came from Healy's plane and the sky was loaded with debris.

No time to think about that now! "Ball turret! 11 o'clock low! Vowels, get the bastard!" yelled Johnson.

"No shouting on the intercom!" barked Tex. "Call out those fighters and stay calm. We'll come out of this all right. Stay calm, and concentrate. Do your job, boys, as you were trained to do."

"Thirty seconds to bombs away, Captain, target looks clear."

As I searched for more fighters, I heard Donovan say, "The lead ship just dropped...Bombs away!"

"OK boys, we're heading home. Navigator, give me a heading," said Tex.

"Yes, sir," I acknowledged, and quickly started plotting our return.

As I was just finishing up, the waist gunner said, "Jameson's right wing is smoking and on fire!" I looked out my window just in time to see three chutes as the plane rolled over and started a steep dive. A few seconds later I saw the ship blow up. Dropping back in my chair I thought how close that was. Our good luck, I guess. Shaking my head back and forth to clear my mind I started looking for fighters once again. *Come on, you sons-of-bitches, come on back.* But by that time the fighting had subsided and we were heading home, yet still on the alert.

Once we reached the Channel, we could relax a little. After reporting our position to Tex, he said it was OK to come off oxygen. I slowly unstrapped my mask, still thinking of Jameson's crew. Who survived and who made it, if you can call becoming a prisoner of war surviving? At that moment I swore I would not become a prisoner under any circumstances.

Once we landed and shut off the engines I started to shake all over again. I sat for a moment to regain my wits. This, I thought, would pass and hopefully become easier with each mission. I had twenty-four more to go.

At de-briefing I learned that the bombardier on Dick Healy's ship was blown through the Plexiglas nose and fell back through one of the engines. One of the navigators fell out of the nose immediately while the other one was hanging on to his navigator's table as he tried to hook back up to oxygen with his free hand. When he let loose he was swept under the aircraft. He was not wearing a parachute. (Many times there were two navigators assigned to the lead ship to avoid any mistakes reaching the target.) At last sighting, Healy was seen gaining control of his ship and heading south towards Belgium.

I spoke with Tex for a couple of minutes and we then headed for the officers' club and a couple of whiskeys.

After a few drinks, hunger started to set in but I really didn't feel much like eating. My brother Doug had written me while I was back in training to say this was to be expected, and how little food he got by on while in the combat zone. *Another shot or two of booze, a smoke and rest up for the next mission. I hope it will be a few days away. Boy do I feel tired.*

This damaged ship somehow returned from a raid over Cologne,
Germany on October 15, 1944. This occurred a month before my tour
started but damage like this was all too common. It's remarkable to me
that some of our pilots were able to maintain control, especially when the
oxygen system was destroyed and portable bottled oxygen was all that
was left and below zero degree winds rushed through the nose at gale
force, but they did. The navigator on this flight survived but the bombardier was killed. One of the navigators on Healy's ship was not so
lucky. This picture not only shows the skill of the pilot—in this case, 1st
Lt. Lawrence De Lancy—but also of the remarkable strength of the B-17.
Photo courtesy of the National Archives.

NOVEMBER 27, 1944

Mission #2

Destination: Offenburg

Target: Railroad Marshalling Yard

I found myself just dozing off when again a flashlight was shining in my face.

"Sir, sir, time to get up sir, another mission today," the orderly beckoned.

"What! Are you kidding me? I just fell asleep!"

"Yes sir, breakfast at 0400, briefing at 0445," muttered the clerk as he was hustling out the door.

Tex was already half-dressed as I started to unravel the blankets.

"Something bothering you, Eddie?"

"No, just a dream. Not worth talking about. Do you think maybe we'll get some real eggs and bacon this morning?"

"Who knows? But the toast and coffee will be good. Come on, let's get moving and get this over with," Tex said, motioning with his arm.

"Today's mission, gentlemen is a railroad marshalling yard at Offenburg, Germany," the briefing officer said as the drapes over our wall map opened.

As we headed for Krautville in formation at 20,000 feet, I thought again of Dick Healy's crew, in particular the two navigators, Billy Mylan and Ray Sponner. I had only talked with these fellows a few times in the past couple of weeks but they seemed like good boys. *Damn*, I thought, *I don't even know where they were from or anything about their families. Oh well, shake it off. There is nothing I can do about it now. Tex was right, I guess, when it's your time, it's your time; nothing you can do to change that.*

For my second mission we had a new co-pilot and a new waist gunner. Changing crews or ships was necessary at times because of casualties but that didn't make it any less unnerving. *I hope they don't bring us bad luck.* Most fellows believed in luck but I tried not to give it much thought. As long as these fellows knew what they were doing and we each covered the other's back we didn't need any luck. I hoped!

Seven and a half hours later we touched down at Molesworth. This mission went well. We made it to the target without seeing any enemy. Probably yesterday's mission had something to do with it. Sixty-seven German aircraft were destroyed with two probable and eleven damaged. Maybe the Germans were learning their lesson.

At de-briefing, I was in better shape. No more shaking. Strangely or perhaps necessarily, yesterday's mission and deaths were quickly fading. *Maybe I can catch up on my eating this evening.*

The next morning, November 28, I automatically awoke to darkness. No flashlights, thank God. I hoped I wasn't dreaming. "Tex," I whispered, "mission today?"

"Naw, get some shut-eye, will ya?" he answered.

The day was spent reviewing our first two missions; what we did right, what we did wrong, what we could do better. The talk around the base was about England's great warrior, General Montgomery and his attack plan of dropping ground troops into Holland. Known as Operation Market Garden, if successful, it could have broken Germany's back and forced her surrender. But it failed miserably.

We flyboys were now going to have to fly more often and deeper into Germany than ever before. Germany was not yet defeated. *I guess we will know pretty soon just how beat they really are, or aren't.*

This is the waist gunner's position—Henja's place.
It got awfully cold back there. Photo courtesy of the National Archives.

These are our "Little Friends" the P-51s. Thank goodness we had them along. Flying eight-hour missions was bad enough, but these guys did it all on their own as pilot, navigator and gunner. At least we could stretch our legs. The boys flying B-17s on missions in 1943, without P-51 escorts, were not as lucky as we were and suffered many more times the losses. Photo courtesy of the National Archives.

NOVEMBER 29, 1944

Mission #3

Destination: Merseburg

Target: Synthetic Oil Refinery

November 29, my third mission, was a run on a synthetic oil refinery at Merseburg, Germany.

What worried us most about this target were those 500-plus, eighty-eight-millimeter anti-aircraft guns. These weapons could cut a squadron to pieces. We all had the intelligence and knew Merseburg was one of the most heavily defended areas in the Third Reich. Since the spring of 1944, the production of these synthetic oil fields had been reduced by as much as seventy-five percent. Germany, in an effort to protect these fields, had reinforced the area and those German gunners really knew how to zero in on our ships.

We had the same crew as our last mission. I guess our two replacements did OK but then again, we didn't have the resistance we had our first time out. At breakfast Haynes, our new co-pilot, started to open up, and spoke of his wife and daughter. He seemed like a nice guy. *He'll fit in.*

We encountered a large number of enemy fighters this time but, in fact, the enemy encountered a large number of us, too. We had nearly a thousand P-51s covering our bombers and boy, was I glad of it. A few German fighters broke through to give us a scare but didn't get close enough to do any damage.

"Yes sir, this flight was OK. Maybe I'll get through this war and back home without too much trouble."

"Don't get used to it," Donovan said. "It never gets easy. We'll revisit Merseburg again, I guarantee it. Those damn Germans know how to clean up and re-start production faster than hell."

Merseburg had over 500 anti-aircraft guns. These black puffs of smoke are flak bursts: each one capable of bringing down a ship. Photo courtesy of the National Archives.

Losses like this B-17 over Merseburg were not uncommon. The entire front of the plane was blown off killing the pilot, co-pilot, navigator and bombardier instantly. The others died also. Sometimes it's best this way— at least you don't have to suffer. Photo courtesy of the National Archives.

NOVEMBER 30, 1944

Mission #4

Destination: Merseburg

Target: The Leuna Synthetic Oil Refinery

How he knew—Donovan, that is—I'll never know, but sure enough at our briefing on November 30 the mission was again Merseburg; and another synthetic oil refinery at Zeitz. Looks like another seven- to eight-hour flight.

"Three minutes to target, pilot to bombardier, make sure you drop the second the lead ship does," Tex said.

All was quiet until the low muffled sound of flak was heard. Looking out the nose, I thought, *How in the hell are we going to get through that?* Flak started to hit our ship everywhere!

"Oh Lord, get us out of here!" I heard Vowels yell. What a place to be, in that cramped ball turret. Vowels had to sit with his knees nearly up to his face for all but a few minutes of flying. Most men would not trade places with him for anything.

Suddenly our ship lurched upward and I came out of my chair.

"What the hell was that?" yelled Tex.

"Sir, there's a hole in our wing the size of a football!" shouted Vowels.

"We're losing fuel!" Haynes shouted.

Shrapnel hitting our ship sounded like rocks hitting a car. The pinging was all around us. I don't mind admitting, this stuff scared the hell out of me.

I heard Tex give the order to our engineer, Sprague, to get to the fuel transfer pump and save some. "Eddie, give him some help! We need to save as much fuel as we can!"

"Yes sir," I shouted, grabbing my portable oxygen tank and making my way to the bomb bay. Sprague had almost finished the work when a flak explosion threw both of us backward. Sprague looked at me as if I had been hit. I thought I was wounded. I felt for my arms and legs, then my chest and face to make sure I was all there. I could not feel any pain or see any blood. I was OK. What the hell was he thinking? Sprague, getting tired from pumping fuel from one tank to another motioned me to take over. I finished the job and radioed to Tex, "Fuel transfer complete, Lieutenant."

"Good, get back to your positions fast," he returned.

"Bombs away!" shouted Donovan. "Bomb bay doors closing," he finished.

"OK boys; let's get the hell away from here. Eddie, give me a heading and get us out of this hell hole," Tex ordered.

"Yes sir, turn to heading three two zero, we'll make a beeline for home, should be back in three and a half hours."

"OK, boys, keep your eyes peeled; Jerry is still out there." However, no fighters were spotted, thanks again to our little friends.

At de-briefing I swore every one of those German eighty-eights were aimed at our ass. There were over thirty-three battle-damaged aircraft from this raid alone, and two men were wounded.

"How in the world could we not lose any aircraft or men with so many weapons firing at us?" I asked the de-briefing officer.

"I don't know, Lieutenant, seems like luck to me," he said off-handedly. "You should get some rest now, Lieutenant; I heard from a 'little birdie' you're returning to Merseburg again tomorrow."

I thought, *OK, then let's get the hell over there and get the God damn job done once and for all!* Most of the guys wanted to finish this mess and start hitting Berlin, better known as "Big B."

Well, we did not return to Merseburg the next day but on December 2 we raided the railroad yards at Oberlahnstein. After that the weather moved in and we were grounded for a day.

I learned that the oil plants at Merseburg and Zeitz, some twenty miles south, were getting the hell kicked out of them. This was the sixteenth bombing mission to those areas and the plants were now about eighty-seven percent destroyed. The Third Division on two raids to those targets on November 25 and 30 had twenty-nine heavies lost to flak, and 290 men.

On the last raid, the First Air Division was to attack Zeitz, and the Third Division, Merseburg. Both were following the same route and were to separate over Osnabruck but the First Division screwed up and overshot this point, while the Third Division followed.

It was fifteen miles before the Third Division realized what had happened and then, after correcting course to get to their target at Merseburg, ran smack dab into the guns of Zeitz.

With Merseburg so heavily protected, the Third Division ended up on the bomb run for about eighteen minutes and was subjected to a mass concentration of fire. This fatal mistake resulted in eighty percent of the Division's planes damaged. So as I said earlier, *Let's get going and get the damn job done.*

Bombs away with only meager flak.
Photo courtesy of the National Archives.

359th Bomb Squadron. Mission: Soest, 12/4/44.
Henry Embrey, Pilot. Photo courtesy of the National Archives and the
303rd Bomb Group Assocition.

DECEMBER 4, 1944

Mission #6

Destination: Soest

Target: Railroad Marshalling Yard

I was wide awake, sweating again over the same damn dream when the orderly clerk came in to awaken us. "Sorry sir, I didn't realize you were already awake. Mission today, breakfast at 0430 and briefing at 0530. You'll wake the others?"

Tex and Donovan were also up but Haynes, our co-pilot, was dead to the world in his own dream mission. "Eugene, let's go, mission today."

The drapes were drawn back and the red line was pointing to a railroad marshalling yard at Soest, Germany, just a few miles southeast of Hamm.

On our way to the equipment room the cold was noticeably worse. I was about to freeze; good thing I was wearing three layers of clothing.

"OK boys, here we go," announced Tex.

As he pushed the throttles forward, our war bird slowly moved into proper position. We waited for a slight fog to pass. The runway was pretty wet and the ship seemed a little slow. As we started to inch off the ground I was wondering what could be holding us back. Could we have ice on the wings? Just then I saw the power lines ahead.

"Pull up, pull up!" I shouted to Tex. "Pull up, pull up!" I shouted again, "Tex, pull up God damn it!" Then Tex dropped the nose!

I fell back against my seat. I pushed my legs against the table braces and grabbed on to anything I could. As soon as I thought we were going in for sure, Tex raised the nose of the plane and barely passed over those lines. *Damn*, I thought to myself, *That was close!* "Navigator to pilot; Tex, how in the hell did we miss that?"

"I had to pick up speed, Eddie, to get the nose up. The only way I could do that was to dive the plane and slingshot up and over. Scared the hell out of you, didn't it?" he offered with a snicker.

The whole crew was quiet for a while. That was too close; cables had caused more than one ship to go down, killing the crew. If I had to die for my country, I didn't want it to be because of some low-hanging electrical cables.

Because of the weather we were delayed forming our groups for about an hour. We all wondered about our fuel situation, especially with an eight-plus-hour mission ahead of us.

"Sir, flak ahead," mentioned Donovan.

"Eddie, give me a time to target."

"Yes sir, about eight and a half minutes, sir," I replied.

"Get ready, Donovan, I'll let you know when we're two minutes away from the target. Get your flak suits on boys, this looks messy," Tex ordered.

I quickly wrapped my flak suit around me and put on my flak helmet. The dark cloudbursts ahead seemed pretty thick. These shell bursts mixed in with the dark clouds were making the distinction between the two nearly impossible.

"Sir, two and a half minutes to target."

"Bombardier, take your position," Tex responded to Donovan.

I was ready to get blasted but something was wrong, no shells were bursting. The groups in front must have knocked out some ground batteries or at least made the Jerrys below run for cover. Good, although I knew the return trip could be bad. I learned sometime ago not to take things like a pause in anti-aircraft fire for granted.

On the return trip Tex radioed that a number of planes in the bomber groups were running low on fuel, forcing landings at some friendly bases in France and Belgium.

"Eddie, give me a check on headwinds, current location and a time of arrival."

"Sir. We're seventy-five miles west of our turning point. Headwind speed of forty knots. Come to heading two niner zero and we should arrive back at base by 0330. We should have enough fuel, sir."

"Thanks. Pilot to crew, keep an eye out for enemy fighters. We have a ways to go boys, before we're out of trouble. Eddie, let me know as soon as we get close to the Channel. We may have to get rid of some weight to make it back."

I knew then we could be in for a tight ride back but I also knew that Tex and Haynes were a couple of first-rate pilots.

"Sir, I just heard from Lieutenant O'Leary. His ship is turning south toward Belgium; they're running low on fuel and don't want to risk a flight all the way back to England," Prehatny, our radio operator said.

"Any others?" Tex asked.

"Yes sir, Lieutenant Juns from the 360th is going to follow O'Leary. A number of other ships from the other three squadrons are also heading to France, sir," answered Prehatny.

"Eddie, double-check your calculations, we need to be right on this one," Tex ordered.

"Yes sir, I have done that and triple-checked sir. If the fuel load is correct we will be back at 0330." Tex knew that I knew my navigation but I could sense a lot of uneasiness with the crew. There was much chatter on the intercom about the dozen or more ships leaving formation for fuel stops. I was sure Tex wanted the rest of the crew to hear our conversation to help calm their nerves.

As we approached the Channel, the order was given to get rid of all unnecessary weight including guns, ammo, flak jackets and helmets. Our ship was as light as it was going to get.

"Eddie, how do we look?"

"Good sir, keep current heading and Molesworth will be just ahead."

Low cloud cover was ahead but patchy; we should be OK, I thought. Tex ordered, "take your positions for landing boys; we'll be down in ten minutes."

In the instant we touched down, the number three engine started to sputter out of fuel but we were on the ground and home safe with no injuries. Tex was cutting it close but he knew what he was doing. The rest of the crew were likewise confident in our pilot's judgment but had they known we were that low, and were it up to a vote, they may have asked him to follow the other planes for an early refueling. What they didn't know was Tex's reluctance to land our ship anywhere danger or trouble could exist. And that could be anywhere outside of England. Hell, earlier in the war some enemy fighters followed our planes over the Channel and fired on them as they were landing!

At de-briefing we learned we would be standing down until the weather cleared. That was fine with me; I could use a little rest. Besides, like Tex and the others I felt it was certainly better here at base than stranded in some other damned country.

After a shower and a meal I headed to the mail shack. Finally, two letters from home. Betty June's letter was sure nice to read. She was doing fine but really worried about me. I sat down and wrote to her.

December 4, 1944

Dear Darling,

I just received your letter and am happy to have finally received it. Everything here is going well. A few close calls but that is to be expected. Our pilot just got us back from a long mission and we will be waiting for better weather before going again. I hope you are well. I miss you very much. I think of the days we spent together back home walking the beach. It's such a contrast over here. The cold is much worse than I thought it would be. I'm always cold. This cold cuts right through you and I'm not sure if I will ever warm up. The ration of coal for our small heater is not enough to last the week and we are always trying to beg, borrow and steal more. Yesterday I traded three packs of my prized Lucky Strikes for five pounds of coal. I sleep with nine blankets and still wake up shivering. Anyway this will pass soon and I will be home and in your warm arms. I miss you.

All my love always,
Edward

December 4, 1944

Dear Dad and Mother,

Please send me a couple of boxes of chocolates, I am sure wanting some. Tell Doug to write. I worry about things as I left them at home. Never change anything. Most of all for Betty June to be as she's always been.

Good, clean, kind, and true to me. I want to marry her as
you know and will if she is as she was six months ago.
Love to all.

Your son,
Edward

The next day we spent mostly in the officers' club playing poker,
having a few drinks and talking of our missions. Some boys were
speculating as to why we were not seeing many Jerry fighters.

"It has to be because we're destroying all the refineries around
Merseburg and some factories responsible for building fighters,"
said a pilot from another ship.

"I'm not so sure," said another, "maybe Jerry is socked in as we
are or maybe they're waiting to put up a few hundred all at once."

"Nonsense," injected Donovan, "we're just kicking their asses!"

"Don't throw in Jerry's towel too fast," a voice from the corner
table said. "The fight's not over until the final bell."

How true, I thought. *I wonder what is up with those bastards.*
"Pass me another beer will ya, Mack?" I said as I folded and threw
in my poker hand.

This B-24 took a direct flak hit over Merseburg.
Photo courtesy of the National Archives.

DECEMBER 6, 1944

Mission #7

Destination: Merseburg, Again

Target: The Leuna Synthetic Oil Plant

The cold was awful the night of December 5. I have never been so miserable. I shivered all night, tossing and turning; trying to stay warm. I was almost glad when the orderly clerk woke me at 0330.

"Mission today, gentlemen. Briefing at 0430."

"The mission for today, gentlemen, is the Leuna synthetic oil plant at Merseburg, Germany. This will be your primary target. We'll put up thirty-nine crews. The secondary target—in the event cloud cover obscures the primary—will be the oil factories at Zeitz. The last resort target will be the marshalling yard in Nordhausen but only if the cloud cover over the primary and secondary is one hundred percent. We will bomb even with a 9/10 cloud cover. Also gentlemen...listen up! All fliers will now have to complete thirty missions to return home, no longer twenty-five."

The room went silent. Not a word. How in the hell did they expect any of us to survive even twenty-five missions, when the average life expectancy for a crewmember was fifteen missions in 1943? Now in 1944 there was a four percent casualty rate with each mission! Everyone knew how to multiply. On average, our chances of making it through twenty-five missions were zero! Were they out of their damn collective minds? I woke up this morning ready to fly my seventh mission with eighteen to go; now I had twenty-three more to go. *Goddamn* I thought, *twenty-three more to go.* Tex, Haynes, Donovan and I all searched each other's faces for answers, but an astounded silence was all we could muster.

At the equipment room the boys were incredulous, cursing the top brass! Since Jerry was not sending up as many fighters, we figured we must be doing them in. The thought of ending this war by Christmas was a real possibility, we were told. Well, the top brass was not flying through flak at Merseburg! What kind of fools did they think we were?

By the time we were over the English Channel three planes had turned back: one had engine problems, one had a runaway prop and one had a sick co-pilot. *Hell, we're all sick!*

The cloud cover was nearly 10/10 in the target area, topping out at 16,000 feet. It was clear flying above that altitude but the enemy flak had us zeroed in. How could they miss our positions with the vapor trails following our planes showing Jerry our exact location? These contrails are a sure giveaway.

"Anybody see any fighters?" the tail gunner asked.

"Negative, not yet anyway," someone answered. Then the explosions began, burst after burst.

The flak hitting our ship was like a thousand hammers pounding on metal. The banging of equipment as the metal fireballs cut through our nose compartment was causing everyone to wonder if we had any of that damn luck everybody talked about.

"Bombs away," shouted Donovan.

"Eddie, give us a heading," Tex ordered in return.

Within minutes we were flying as fast as we could, turning left, then right, changing altitude, going up, down, trying to evade more flak.

After Tex brought us in safely to base, we waited around for a couple of stragglers. We didn't want any more casualties.

"There she is!" shouted someone behind us. "Over there!"

We looked up to see a ship turning on its downwind leg and then to its final approach. A flare was fired out of the waist gunner's position. Wounded on board. The rescue and fire vehicles were at the ready. We waited to see where the ship ended up on the runway before heading over to lend a hand.

"There's the other ship!"

"Another flare!"

After the two ships had landed and come to a safe stop, we ran over to help out, all the while hoping the killed or wounded did not include a buddy.

As I arrived, one medic was wrapping blankets around a wounded gunner while another was holding a bottle of plasma above the stretcher.

"Anything I can do to help, Doc?" I asked.

"No sir, Lieutenant, we have everything under control."

Just then a ground-crew sergeant staggered out of the waist gunner's window and fell to the ground heaving up his lunch. The medic glanced over at him then to me and said, "Lieutenant, maybe you can help. Take this blanket and bring this boy's boot out."

"His boot, why do I need a blanket for his boot?" I asked.

"Sir, please, his leg is still in it. Wrap it and bring it over to the ambulance. And hurry, we don't need any more men doing what that guy just did."

I ran to the plane and started looking around. I found the gunner's leg. God, what a mess. I froze momentarily just staring and felt my stomach heave. I wanted to throw up but just couldn't. As I gasped for a quick breath I opened the blanket and carefully scooped the flier's boot, wrapping it as I turned to exit. With a quick step I hurried to the ambulance and carefully laid the bundle under a seat. And as I half walked, half staggered away, I remember thinking, *God, I hope I'll never have to do that or the like ever again. I hope the boy makes it.*

I turned away from the bloody, sickening scene to find Donovan's gaze fixated on my pale, vacant face. "You all right, Eddie?"

"Yeah, I'm OK. Let's go. Let these guys do their job. They're trained for this kind of stuff."

We made our way back to the club, downed a couple of drinks and warmed ourselves by the stove.

The next morning we awoke to bad weather. We knew there wouldn't be any mission today. I noticed Tex already up and dressed.

"What's on your mind, kid?" Tex asked, finally breaking the silence.

"Nothing but that same damn dream…I can't forget it."

"Thought for once you were sleeping soundly; didn't hear you talking in your sleep for a change," Tex remarked.

These guys who were bunked around me for the last month had complained about my constant talking in my sleep, always about our missions or some combat event.

"Come on, give. Why does this dream bother you so much?" Tex asked again.

Bother me?! Does he think I want to talk about it now? I took another second and said, "Forget it." I quickly dressed and left the hut. I don't know what had gotten into me, but I couldn't sit there any more. Besides, I was ready to get some of my beloved coffee.

The news came down that we were not going on any mission that day, as we expected, and from the weather forecast it looked like we would be socked in for a few days. I thought maybe this would be a good time to get a jeep and head to London for a night or two. Change the scenery, visit some bars, dance, have some fun and forget about this war. Get back to some normal living for a change, or close to normal, anyway.

It snowed all that day and most of the night. The snowplows were useless. All we could do was try and stay warm. Maybe the next day we could get to London.

DECEMBER 11, 1944

Mission #8

Destination: Mannheim

Target: Railroad Bridge

London was not to be. The weather had tied us to the base for four days. On the fifth day the weather cleared and we were given orders to bomb a railroad bridge at Mannheim, Germany. Mannheim was almost as far south as Stuttgart and was therefore to be an eight-hour mission. The briefing officer spoke up:

"Gentlemen, today's mission will consist of the largest fleet of bombers ever assembled. Crews will total 15,900 men with an aircraft column stretching over 100 miles. B-24s will be flying with our 17s. Eight-hundred-fifty P-51 Mustang fighters will escort the fleet. Good luck, gentlemen."

Our bomb group was to dispatch the second largest number of B-17s during the war. We totaled fifty-two planes. The ground crews worked long and hard, day and night, to get the bombers ready. Our crew chief was the best mechanic I have ever known. If a slight odd sound was heard, Ed was able to locate it and have us underway without missing a beat. I just don't know how he identified some of the problems he did. So far, we had flown every bombing run without having to turn back once due to mechanical problems.

"Bombardier, watch the lead ship. We need to make sure we drop when they do," Tex announced.

The sky ahead was beautiful, as blue as it could be with a few lazy clouds spread around. No enemy fighters to be seen. I was thinking this was too good to be true and was about to mention this fact to Tex when I saw a ship coming straight for us.

"Pull up! Tex, pull up! Ship ahead!"

Within a matter of a split second I thought we were goners. Tex dove our ship as the one coming head-on lifted! A close call. A few minutes later Lieutenant Harding's plane and his crew were not so lucky.

Our base at Molesworth. In the background are bombers lining up for
Mannheim. Photo courtesy of the National Archives.

My heart was pumping a mile a minute and my hands would not stay still. *Boy, would I like a smoke right now!* Then I saw Lieutenant Harding's plane, "Thunderbird," burst into flames. Everything happened so fast I could not tell if it was flak or a midair collision. "What happened to Harding's ship? Did anyone see?" I asked over the intercom. "Any chutes?"

"He hit another ship returning from their drop," Haynes answered.

"Keep your eyes peeled, everyone!" Tex ordered. "This isn't over yet!"

Harding was a good pilot and his navigator, Garvey, had been in my class. Both were good men.

"Any chutes?" Tex repeated. But before he could get an answer the plane next to us was hit and was pulling out of formation.

"That's *Forget Me Not Olly*, Lieutenant Bixby's ship," Haynes blurted out.

Not Bixby, I thought. Two ships hit on either side of us. Gone. Harding's crew lost; no chutes reported. Hell, they didn't even have time to know what happened.

"Somebody watch Bixby's ship; let me know if she is going down or heading for the clouds," Tex commanded.

"It looks like she is heading for cloud cover, sir," replied Bartkowski, our tail gunner.

"Bombs away," Donovan said lightly.

"Course three one zero, sir," I gave to Holmes.

As we turned I made my way up to the cockpit for a much-needed look at some different scenery.

Haynes was now flying the plane. It was unusual for a co-pilot to be taking over the craft so soon. I looked over at Tex. He was sweating heavily while wiping his brow with his forearm. "Tex, you OK?" I asked.

"Sure, Eddie, sure. Just a little bug, I think. Flu maybe."

Haynes glanced over at me and motioned with his head to get back to my position. I understood without a word passing between us. As I rechecked our position I realized that even a tough man like Tex could be shaken up. Lieutenant Harding was a close friend of his and I knew he would take this one harder than the others. Not to mention having just flown straight through heavy flak, unable to take any evasive action. It's a tough thing to keep your poise when someone is shooting at you and you cannot shoot back. I was glad that I turned out to be a navigator and not a pilot. Being behind the controls was not as glamorous and romantic as it was cracked up to be.

The long return trip was solemn and eerily quiet. The only interruptions were for positions and to make ready for landing. Even our happy-go-lucky waist gunner, Sergeant Hejna, was quiet all the way back.

No one felt much like eating or drinking that evening. The thought of ten more footlockers being cleaned out, ten more buddies killed, was rough on all of us. This was only my eighth mission. Twenty-two more to go—Jesus! All of us thought the missions would be getting a little easier from here out. We were wrong.

Midair collisions meant instant death. This cloud of debris only a moment ago was a ship with ten American flyboys. Photo courtesy of the National Archives.

Often men were not able to escape their ship, becoming trapped by the centrifugal force of the spin. Some of the worst sounds we ever heard over our radio were the screams of those crewmembers as their ships disappeared into the clouds.
Photo courtesy of the National Archives.

The bombardier had some great views in clear weather. This is Donovan's position. I am right behind him. Photo courtesy of the National Archives.

DECEMBER 12, 1944

Mission #9
Destination: Merseburg
Target: The Leuna Synthetic Oil Refinery

The mission was once again the Leuna synthetic oil refinery at Merseburg.

I hoped not to have a repeat of the previous day's mission. Our pilots, Tex and Haynes, both seemed OK at briefing and breakfast. This morning Tex ate some of those powdered eggs and Spam with his toast, jelly and coffee. Looks to me like he has already shaken off yesterday's losses and is ready to continue the fight.

At briefing we were told that if we were on target today, it would be our final mission to the Leipzig area. "This will be the eighteenth and final mission for the Eighth Air Force to the oil refinery at Leuna today, gentlemen. This target has cost us 119 heavy bombers and nearly 1200 men killed, captured or wounded. Let's all get back today and finally finish up with this hell hole."

Our bomb group, the 303rd, lost six of those aircraft on a total of eight missions over this area. I for one was damn glad to be moving on to other targets; hopefully ones that didn't have some 500 anti-aircraft guns zeroed in on us, like we were facing over Merseburg.

On the return flight I thought, *What a difference a day makes. Today, no enemy fighters.* The bits of aluminum foil (called chaff) dropped to jam the enemy's radar seemed to work well this time. Only four ships had minor flak damage.

At de-briefing, while we waited for reports of our strike, we learned that "The Floose" of the 358th bomb squad had just completed its 100th successful combat mission, the first of the 303rd Bomb Group's planes to do so. *That's a lot of flying and a lot of luck*, I thought.

We were informed that our results today were nearly eighty percent successful, which should reduce the oil output at Merseburg to ten percent or less. This damned place was now finished and not worth bombing any more. Thank God!

The next four days we spent on base resting because of the bad weather. It's just fine to take a day or two off but after four days or so many of us get restless. The practical jokes some of the fellows play on the others can cause short tempers, and more than one scuffle broke out. We all knew what the problem was.

At mess hall this afternoon conversations were about flying in all kinds of weather, good or bad. We all just wanted to finish our jobs and get home.

That night I had one of the best night's sleep I have had in weeks. My only problem was getting to chow before the mess hall closed. After breakfast some of us learned that the Germans were beginning an offensive. Some Nazi general, named von Rundstedt, was pushing hard in the Ardennes.

Naturally, we were anxious to hear what was going on in the ground war. We knew that we could not provide air support for our guys because of the crummy weather, which made us madder than hell. It was like we were all sitting around some fished-out little pond. We knew we weren't going to catch any fish, yet there we sat with our lines in the water, waiting for a nibble.

The CO walked in and started to tell us what was going on. "Gentlemen, the Germans have broken through our lines and as best as we can figure, the Krauts are trying to break our army in two. That's all I know at this point except all leave is cancelled. Be ready to fly at a moment's notice."

"Obviously, this weather is shielding the German advance," Haynes offered. "What's bad for us has been good for our enemy. Damn it to hell!"

The news was scarce at the time and we all wondered how big a push this was. How many German divisions were involved, and how close to our troops were they? *If the weather clears soon, I hope we can blow the hell out of them without having any friendly fire casualties.*

More "Little Friends," P-47s flying along with and protecting the 95th Bomb Group. Photo courtesy of the National Archives.

This is the lead crew on our raid to Koblenz on December 18, 1944.
This raid turned out to be a milk run. We had over 100 "Little Friends"
escorting us. Photo courtesy of the National Archives and the 303rd
Bomb Group Association.

DECEMBER 18, 1944

Mission #10

Destination: Koblenz

Target: Railroad Marshalling Yards

On the morning of December 18 we were told to suit up and get ready to go. Our target: the railroad marshalling yards at Koblenz.

On the way over, nothing new happened. A few enemy fighters were quickly taken care of by our "little friends," the P-51s. Only a few scattered flak bursts in the distance were observed. In fact, on the journey home, we finally learned first-hand what a "milk run" was; no enemy fighters and very minimal, if any, flak; no casualties and all planes returning home. If the German offensive was as big as some had said, Hitler must be using most of his remaining resources for this one last, great push.

At de-briefing we were told our bombing results went unobserved, as the cloud cover was 10/10 most of the way in and after the drop. In fact many planes were diverted to airfields in Cornwall, Wales or other places north. We were socked in for days waiting for the weather to clear.

We learned the Germans had twenty-five divisions in the Eifel, across from the Ardennes. "How in the hell could that be?" I asked. "How could so many troops move so far with supplies without anyone being aware?" What happened to our intelligence? We had knocked out most of their oil refining capabilities at Merseburg. Just where was their gas supply coming from? There had to be a real intelligence screw-up somewhere. While we were sleeping the enemy was making this big surprise move that could result in the deaths of thousands of our boys; and we are stuck here not able to do a damn thing about it!

Koblenz was my tenth mission. I couldn't help but hope that the ones to follow would be similar. Maybe I could complete the remaining twenty missions without too much trouble.

Some of the fellows and I decided to head to London for a little fun. Tex, Donovan and I were feeling no pain one night when we decided to try another bar. We were feeling pretty happy and full of ourselves, staggering from one pub to another when I spotted a couple of flyboys across the street. We decided to investigate. Three MPs were telling them to get inside the pub, leave or be arrested. Not knowing who started what, I thought I would just let it go and continue my fun.

"Where you headed, Lieutenant?" asked this giant of an MP, with a hint of indignation.

This guy must have been about six-foot four, two-hundred-fifty pounds!

"I'm headed where I'm headed," I snapped back. I didn't care how big he was. This behind-the-scenes MP wasn't doing any fighting. He was nothing to me. Most servicemen buckled under to MPs because they didn't want to be thrown in the guardhouse.

I turned and began walking away when this fellow ordered, "Stop right there, Lieutenant. I said, where are you headed?"

I turned and looked him in the eye but before I could tell him where to go he said, "Do you think I give a damn about you flyboys, how tough you are, how many missions you've flown?" He pulled up his shirt and said, "You see these scars, buddy? A German machine gun damn near tore me in half. Now answer my question!"

I was drunk but not so drunk to realize this guy had seen his share of action and could take care of me with one swing. "Back to the base, I guess."

"Tuck in your shirt and straighten your tie and get lost!" He ordered.

"Whatever you say; I'm on my way...." Just as well, not getting the hell kicked out of me.

"I didn't want to hurt the guy," I said to Tex and Donovan with a wink. "Let's go."

DECEMBER 27, 1944

Mission #11

Destination: Euskirchen

Target: Railroad Yards

After nine days of down time, which was unusual, we were assigned to bomb a railroad yard at Euskirchen, Germany. We had to knock out as many of the supply lines that fed the German war machine as possible. No gas, no fighting, was our mantra.

By this time we had learned that the 82nd and 101st Airborne divisions were at a place named Bastogne and were cut off from supplies. Their ammo, food and worst of all, clothing, were in short supply. With the freezing weather from one of the worst winters in recent European history, these boys had to be suffering. They had been fighting since D-Day and obviously were a real tough bunch. Hopefully they could hold out.

Flying above the battle line near St. Vith, the skies were calm; no enemy fighters, which was just as well, for none of our little friends were around either. Once we got close to the front lines of the Battle of the Bulge, however, all hell broke loose!

"Flak burst, 12 o'clock!" Donovan shouted.

"Two minutes to bomb run. Donovan, keep your eye on the lead ship. Make sure we drop with them. Get ready boys, things look pretty busy ahead," said Tex.

He wasn't kidding! "Son of a bitch!" I shouted. "Get your battle suits on fellas, we're heading right to it."

"I thought all this stuff was behind us when we destroyed Merseburg," Vowels said.

Flak was pinging our ship and piercing our nose. "Damn, that's close!" I shouted.

Donovan was watching through the Plexiglas nose to make sure he dropped when the lead ship dropped its bombs. How he could keep calm always surprised me, especially when chunks of hot metal were flying all around and inside our ship. His concentration served us and the effort well.

"Damn, Roger's plane is on fire, he's turning ahead of us."
Photo courtesy of the National Archives.

This is Bartkowski's territory. Twin 50-calibers would tear those enemy
planes apart. "Bart" fooled many an enemy fighter.
Photo courtesy of the National Archives.

"Where are our little friends when we need them? I know we are going to catch hell after bombs away and start our turn for home." I heard someone say.

"I bet they are strafing ground targets," I heard Haynes answer. "We're over the battle lines boys, and Jerry is concentrated below us."

"Damn, Rogers' plane is on fire, he's turning ahead of us."

"Bombs away!" announced Donovan as he sat back, reflecting on the devastation he had unleashed below. "Bomb bay doors closing."

I watched Donovan slowly wiping his hands as if to wash them of the blood to be spilled below. *So what the hell, I thought, England has had its cities pummeled and thousands of her citizens murdered by these bastards. I don't feel sorry for any of them. If this is what we have to do to end this mess, so be it; the sooner the better.* Donovan grabbed his weapon and was looking for fighters when he turned towards me and gave me the thumbs up, a sign of a good hit on the target.

"Navigator, where's that heading? We need to get the hell out of here," Tex said.

"Sir, here sir. Turn to two two zero. We can skirt around some of the flak by going south of the lines. This way considering our fuel supply, we can make it back safely although a little later than expected," I responded.

"Did anyone see what happened to Lieutenant Rogers' ship?"

"Yes, sir" Bartkowski answered. "He's behind us now and falling in with some of the other flights. He's keeping up with them. Maybe he'll make it, sir."

Being in the tail gunner's position, Bartkowski had unrestricted views of our targets as they were hit, and many of the planes and the action going on. Although this was a great place to observe, it was a terrible place to be during a raid. More than once, enemy fighters flew behind us in our contrails, hiding until they were within a few hundred yards and then and only then, showing themselves long enough to fire a quick burst or two.

Two missions ago, Bartkowski purposely held his fire when he spotted an Messerschmitt 109 sneaking up in our exhaust clouds. With his gun barrels dropped low the Jerry must have thought the tail gunner was dead and made the fatal mistake of showing himself, getting too close, within a couple hundred yards or so. Boy, I bet he was surprised when the two barrels of Bart's machine guns raised up suddenly, stared squarely at him and let go a barrage of fire. Well, if he had time to realize what was going on before being blown to bits, he'd have been surprised.

"Fighters are going after the low group. Where the hell is our cover?" I heard someone say.

"OK boys, stay alert. We're not out of this yet," Tex ordered.

We were able to evade the worst of the flak and fighters before heading into cloud cover. As we made our way back to Molesworth we were glad to be going home and feeling good about our mission.

At de-briefing, we learned that only five men were wounded, and even though thirty-one aircraft were damaged—seventeen seriously—all birds made it back safely.

The snow was falling again. The wind picked up while we were making our way to the barracks; I knew we would stand down tomorrow.

The next day was so damn cold we all decided to hang out at the officers' club and stay warm on the inside and outside by filling our stomachs with whiskey and huddling around one of the coal stoves. I swore our barracks would be a solid block of ice by the time we returned for some shuteye.

Around 10 P.M. I headed back to the barracks and found I was right. It was so cold inside I didn't bother changing clothes. I just put more on and slid between my nine covers. The last thing I remember thinking before sleep was, *Eleven missions behind me now and only nineteen to go.*

The morning of December 29 we were assigned to bomb a railroad bridge at Bullay, Germany, with secondary targets being the marshalling yard again at Koblenz.

This would be our first mission over the Rhine River. We needed to prevent supplies being shipped to the Jerrys. Bridges are awfully small targets to hit from thousands of feet up, and we would be flying in at 20,000 feet. With our squadron carrying a load of 222 1,000-pound high explosive bombs, we knew a good hit would do the job.

This is a picture of the railroad yard at Essen, Germany,
similar to our target of December 27, 1944 over Euskirchen.
Photo courtesy of the National Archives.

When the snow had us socked in we didn't do much except try to stay
warm by one of our coal stoves, telling jokes and inventing up heroic
tales. Our ration of coal was not enough to keep us warm, so at times
we went on coal "raids" during the night to make sure we had what
we needed. Some mornings we would discover we were also victims
of such raids. Photo courtesy of the National Archives.

The infantry boys of the 82nd and the 101st Airborne Paratroopers were still dug in at Bastogne, and as we understood the 101st was surrounded. The military newspapers described how these boys withstood all German advances and their commander, General McAuliffe, had answered the German Commander's offer to surrender with a one word message: "NUTS!" or in other words, "Go to Hell!"

Soon thereafter, General "Blood and Guts" Patton broke through the German lines to give those boys some relief. The newspapers said Patton rescued them, but somehow we knew those warriors did most of the fighting themselves and deserved what the papers had renamed their outfit: "The Battered Bastards of Bastogne."

Knocking out supply bridges and other targets from the air to slow the enemy and help out those boys dug-in in the frozen dirt and living in the most miserable conditions, reminded me of my school lessons about George Washington's troops at Trenton and Valley Forge. In both of those battles, Americans were wet, cold and hungry. They had little winter clothing; were in fact starving. Many boys had no shoes. At Valley Forge many stood guard duty with their feet inside their hats so they could keep their feet warm.[2] A lot of boys—the first American GIs—lost legs and feet by amputation due to frostbite, but they stayed and fought. They knew what they had to do, just the same as those guys at Bastogne.

The cold we suffered every day at 25,000 feet was bad enough. But if you didn't get killed, wounded or captured, at least you could fly home to some hot coffee, hot meals and a shower. Those boys at Bastogne had to fight it out from frozen foxholes with little or no hot food, clothes or fires. *Yes sir*, I thought, *anything I can do to kill the Hun and help out our boys, the better off we all are.*

The evening of December 30, I had completed my thirteenth mission. I thought I was doomed today because Donovan and I had been assigned to a new crew whose navigator and bombardier had been wounded. This "bad luck" mission aboard the ship *Yankee Doodle II* ended uneventfully. My second "milk run," there was no enemy aircraft and no anti-aircraft fire. I believed Jerry was starting to get beat.

---

[2] A.J. Langguth, *Patriots: The Men Who Started the American Revolution* (New York: Simon & Schuster, 1998), 468

1945

EIGHT MISSIONS IN NINE DAYS

We welcomed in 1945 over our next few missions. They were somewhat routine, if flying into enemy skies, dropping bombs, being shot at from the ground and from the sky can ever be routine. Between December 29 and January 8 we completed eight missions in nine days. The missions were to seven railroad yards and bridges at Euskirchen, Bullay, Kaiserlautern, Neuss, Cologne, Kall and Schweich and an airfield at Nieder-Breisig, all in Germany. On the mission to Neuss, I flew in one of my favorite planes, the *Forget Me Not Olly*. We did not see many fighters or close flak, but what we did see were a number of men getting to the point of becoming "flak-happy": shell-shocked, frozen, whatever you want to call it; different wars and different generations have different names for it. The Brits had their own name, LMF, or lacking moral fiber.

I had a chance to talk with a couple of British flyboys a few days earlier. These Brits had their own heavy bombers; the Lancaster, Stirling, and Halifax. It was hard enough for us to fly daylight raids but these boys did it at night. In the early years of the war, British fighter planes didn't have enough fuel to escort their bombers on such long raids. The bomber pilots took evasive action to dodge enemy fighters and flak guns, making precision bombing impossible. We Americans flew daylight precision raids and even with heavy losses, we could at least see the flak bursts and enemy fighters. They didn't know when a fighter was shooting at them until they saw the fire from the enemy's guns; often times only long enough to realize they were doomed. And they have been fighting the war for six long years with losses of nearly 60,000 airmen; 60,000! Some of them were bound to crack. Hell, some of our own boys cracked.

The worst place for a crackup, obviously, was in the air. At more than one de-briefing we heard stories of men freezing at their post. A few minutes before landing, one pilot became "hypnotized" and put the entire crew in danger by freezing at the stick. The top turret gunner and navigator had to literally pry his hands off the wheel and wrestle him to the floor while the co-pilot gained control of the plane, bringing it to a safe landing.

I had also seen a fellow loading his gear, or should I say, trying to load his gear into the nose of his plane. After tossing it in he grabbed the doorway as he had done many times before; lifting his legs while doing a pull-up and swinging in. Only this time, try as he might, he could not make it all the way. I had heard of this sort of thing before and kept a watchful eye out for it, but this was the first time I had actually witnessed this kind of trancelike state.

We had been instructed that once a man becomes shell-shocked or flak-happy he is no longer any good. This is not to say he has turned coward or afraid. It's just that the body no longer responds. When your mind says no, your body does what it's told and stops functioning. Men get this glazed look in their eyes and seem to be staring miles in the distance not noticing a thing, just staring blankly, seemingly lost.

So I watched this fellow try repeatedly to pull himself up into the plane but always falling short. Finally he seemed to give up and started looking at his hands as if questioning them. I was about ready to tell my pilot when a fellow crewmember hurried to his aid, grabbing his shoulders shaking him, telling him I guess, to get a hold of himself and wake up. Another crewmember came to help but by that time it was too late. This guy had gone over the edge. If he ever got his sanity back I didn't believe he would be allowed to fly again. It was better this way rather than in flight, for God's sake. The stress of the last eight missions in nine days was taking its toll. Spending six to eight hours on your toes at full alert, not knowing when a burst of flak or a lone bullet had your name on it, was gut-wrenching and I, for one, needed some rest.

I witnessed my first belly landing during that time. I stood with Donovan and watched as a plane came in with no landing gear. I instinctively took a step back, knowing that once it hit the ground the pilot would have no control over the direction of the ship. The runway was clear and this bird had all the space it needed. The pilot wisely chose a grassy area next to the concrete landing strip. As he landed and made contact, dirt and debris started flying everywhere. The ship started to turn a little, and plowed through some tents. All of a sudden I thought of the ball turret gunner possibly being stuck in his bubble below the plane. *Was he trapped? Did he have a wife, a sweetheart, a child? My God,* I thought, *what a way to get it. Damn, I hope he made it out.*

This was one wreck where I had to help out. Most guys just stared, then slowly turned and walked away, thankful it wasn't them. I motioned to a couple of fellows to follow me. We made our way to the wreckage expecting the worse. A medic was already on the scene and motioned to us not to bother. "Everyone here is OK!" Thank goodness for that.

On January 9 the weather was terrible but forecasts were for better skies the next day. We were all glad for the lousy weather for two reasons; one, we could catch up on our rest and two, it was the group's 300th mission and we all wanted to be at our best. We were all looking forward to this milestone and for me personally, this would be my nineteenth mission with only eleven more to go before, God willing, heading home. It just didn't seem possible. Hopefully, my luck would hold out although I must admit, I didn't really believe much in that sort of thing.

"Chutes were seen but we don't know how many survived, if any."
Photo courtesy of the National Archives.

JANUARY 10, 1945

Mission #19

Destination: Bonn

Target: Airfield

MY WORST MISSION YET

I awoke to the orderly clerk shining his flashlight in my face as he told me, like so many times before, "Mission today sir, briefing at 0500, breakfast at 0600."

I was up and ready to get this flight over with, after finally having a peaceful night's sleep. Breakfast was a surprise. Real eggs and real bacon and all you could eat. *Where was this coming from?* No matter, it had been a long time since I had some real food and I was glad to eat and enjoy.

After gathering my equipment, I joined Tex and Haynes at the briefing. While relaxing with a smoke, the briefing officer opened the dark curtain. "The target for today gentlemen, Merseburg, in the Leipzig area."

"What?" "No way!" I heard three or four men shout at the same time. "I thought we destroyed that refinery, what's going on?" Our concerns, of course, were all those antiaircraft guns surrounding the refinery.

"Quiet, gentlemen," our officer interrupted. "Jerry has been busy rebuilding and we need to knock it out again. No gas, no war."

The weather was clear at our final turning point, the IP. Just as we turned on our bomb run, I could see that same damn flak exploding ahead. I was flying in the lead plane and knew all planes would drop their bombs as soon as they saw us drop. Knowing those enemy flak guns were targeting us was not very comforting!

"Better get on your flak suits, men," Tex ordered. "Donovan, it's your plane."

The next thing I knew, the plane was shooting upwards! Flak must have hit underneath us!

"Donovan, forget it! I'm flying the plane again," Tex commanded, while switching off the autopilot. Another blast, then another!

"Oh my God, number three is on fire!" shouted Haynes. "Cut fuel, feather prop," were the orders.

I started to remove my flak suit, as did Donovan, and while reaching for my parachute, a loud thunderous blast blew away part of our nose and Donovan was swept out and under the plane.

I grabbed for my table, making sure I still had my chute with my other hand. "What's going on?" I yelled, but heard no reply.

We were starting to fade to the left and slowly nosing down. "We have to level off, we have to level off!" I shouted. What were Tex and Haynes doing?

I managed to crawl to the cockpit and there I found Tex and Haynes, bloody and both slumped over the wheel. I turned to see the top turret gunner, Sprague, also bleeding and not moving. I checked him out: dead also. As I looked to the rear there was no radio, waist or tail gunner! They must have bailed! I turned and headed back to bail out of my hatch, when all of the sudden the ship started in a slow spiral, pinning me against the side wall.

I have to get the hell out of here, I said to myself. *I don't want to die this way!*

As I grabbed and crawled my way to the escape door, another blast hit and I was blown out of the plane. I could no longer hear anything, I could see our ship turning down and heading in.

I was beginning to pass out, since my oxygen mask had been ripped away as I fell. Everything was peaceful now, at least for a few moments, until I came to and saw the ground coming up fast! I reached for my pull ring but my hand was frozen stiff. I could not bend my fingers. I tried and tried until finally I was able to engage my thumb. Grasping and pulling the cord, the chute finally opened. I started to descend much slower. *Oh, God. All the crew is lost. All my friends gone!*

"Get a grip," I told myself out loud. "They're gone, nothing I can do about that now. Get some bearings. Where are the enemy lines?"

I saw a lot of movement below as I drifted towards an open field. If those people are German farmers I could be in for it. They kill flyboys. Better check my forty-fives. I was glad to have both of them with me.

I was landing on the far side of a snow-covered field. I thought I might have a chance if I could make it to the trees. I quickly unharnessed my chute and started for the trees when five or six men appeared from nowhere with rifles and pitchforks.

"Come on, you bastards!" I shouted.

"Ed! Eddie! Wake up!" Tex was raising his voice as he shook my shoulder. "You're having that damn dream of yours! Snap out of it! That's an order!"

My eyes shot open and I gazed around, thinking I had been shot. *What's happening?*

"Eddie, wake up, we have a mission, the group's 300th."

"This dream has to end sooner or later," I murmured.

At breakfast I just could not stomach any more powdered eggs, not now anyway. "Just coffee and toast," I said as I went through the chow line.

"Eddie, what's the dope? What gives with your dream?" Tex asked.

I explained the entire dream to Tex about our ship getting hit and starting to drop and spin and how he and the others were killed. "I hope that's not a premonition of some kind."

Tex just looked at me with a snicker and said, "Me too! Hey, it's just a dream. We all have 'em. Forget about it and do your job. You'll be all right."

"Well, let me say this. If we ever take a hit and start to burn, I'm heading out my escape hatch. I don't want to end up all blood and guts on some other plane's nose."

"Your targets for today gentlemen: Bonn, and Cologne, Germany. I don't have to remind you boys this is our 300th mission, the first such mark reached by any bomb group flying out of England. Let's make this our best run yet. Length of mission is six hours," the briefing officer added.

As we made our way into takeoff position the weather turned worse; winds increased and snow started to swirl and whip around.

As we approached enemy skies, we all knew the Battle of the Bulge was raging below. None of us knew where the battle lines started or ended. We sure didn't want to have to bail out, knowing that if we were captured, we'd probably be shot right then. No Jerry wanted to worry with a flyboy prisoner at this stage of the war.

"Flak ahead boys, suit up," came the order. Tex had to fly straight, as we were just minutes from our drop zone. The flak bursts were looking pretty dead-on accurate.

"Sir, something is wrong, sir. We should be over the target but the lead plane isn't dropping its bombs," Donovan said to Tex.

"Hold up, bombardier. The lead flight is telling us that we are over the wrong target. Too many clouds and snow are making the target obscure. We are going around again."

These are words none of us wanted to hear. Going around for the second time on a bomb run was crazy! It could mean sure death! The Jerrys had more time to zero in on us and knock our ass right out of the sky.

"Look smart boys, we have to hit the target today or come back tomorrow," Tex said.

We were just finishing our 360-degree turn and lining up again on our final run when Tex said, "Hold up! There's a group of B-24s below us and coming across our formation. Orders are to go around again."

"Jesus Christ!" someone shouted. "We're going to get it this time, I just know it! Nobody survives three chances on a bomb run and lives to tell about it!"

"Quiet on the intercom!" Tex yelled. "We're here to bomb an airfield and that's what we're going to do. I don't like it any more than any one of you, but dropping our bombs on empty farmland does no one any good. We have orders and we are going to follow them. Now let's make sure everyone does their job so we can get the hell out of here and back home in one piece."

Boom! Boom! Damn, the bursts were everywhere!

"One of our planes just got it! Is that Gates' ship?" Sprague, our top turret asked.

Haynes immediately answered, "I think so. Keep an eye on him."

As I leaned over to look out the front bubble, our B-17 lurched upward as we took a hit under the nose! "Fire in number three!" shouted Haynes.

"Cut fuel, feather prop!" Tex responded.

"Not working, sir! She's still burning! I'll try the fire extinguisher," Haynes answered. BOOM! Another burst and more bits of metal penetrated the nose.

"B-24s coming in below us. We have to go around again."
Photo courtesy of the National Archives.

Oh, my God, I thought. *This is my dream come true! I've gotta get out of here!*

"Sir, the fire is not going out. Should we jump, sir?" asked the ball turret gunner.

"Stay where you are!" Tex ordered. "Navigator, you OK?"

"Yes, sir," I answered. "But this looks bad."

"You guys stay where you are, I'll get this fire out. Hold on boys!" Tex shouted. "Hold on!"

Tex was pulling us up instead of diving to put out the flames. *What the hell is he doing? I hope he hasn't lost his mind. Holy crap!* We were heading up at least seventy to seventy-five degrees. Everything was falling around me; my maps, compasses, pencils, everything! Donovan was hugging his chair and bracing himself with his feet against my worktable. Just then we were slowing and the plane seemed to stop in midair, then began to slide backwards, falling tail first! Down, down we went. As the nose started to turn left, we started to tumble.

"Fire's out!" shouted Vowels from his turret.

"Looks like she's out!" confirmed Haynes.

"Haynes, Haynes!" yelled Tex, "give me a hand with these controls."

The fire was out but we were starting to spin. I was falling into Donovan as we both started sliding towards the nose heading down! I could hear Tex and Haynes growling as they wrestled with the controls. The noise of our engines under that strain was deafening and I knew something had to give.

"Eighteen thousand, seventeen thousand!" Haynes shouted. We were dropping fast. "Two hundred and forty miles an hour, sir! We're beyond our safe dive speed!"

"Pull up! Pull up you bastard!" Tex growled, as we started to level off, still with a full bomb load.

"Fifteen thousand eight hundred feet, sir," Haynes said with a sigh of relief. "Engine looks OK, sir; all fires out and prop feathered."

"Everyone OK? Check in," ordered Tex.

We tagged onto another group coming up from the rear and dropped on target at Bonn. "Give us a course, Eddie; let's get the hell out of here."

"Chutes were seen but we don't know how many survived, if any."
Photo courtesy of the National Archives.

How Tex was able to pull off that piece of flying I'll never know. A backwards stall extinguishing a fire raging in the back of an engine was beyond belief. *He should get a medal*, I thought.

We were the lucky ones, as we learned at de-briefing. Lieutenant Gates' plane was just ahead of us and we learned he lost three engines to flak fire. Chutes were seen but we didn't know how many survived, if any.

The *Buzz Blonde* piloted by Lieutenant Smith of the 427th Bomb Squadron, collided with another ship just after bombs away. Two chutes were seen as the plane headed down but was still under control. And the famous, *Iza Vailable 111* of the 360th Bomb Squad was rammed in the tail section and had to make an emergency landing somewhere. The tail gunner was seen falling but no chute was seen opening. With that many planes making turns while under fire, it's a wonder any of us made it back.

I thanked Tex for saving our asses and offered to buy him a beer at the officers' club.

"You're on!" he answered. "By the way, Eddie, dreams don't always come true."

Our crew was to stand down for a few days for repairs and bad weather. On January 13 the group was headed for Mannheim, Germany, for its 301st mission. Our plane and crew were not scheduled to go. The crews that did, however, ran into some awful trouble. After the 300th mission with all its foul-ups, the crews were ready to get things right. No more "FUBAR," we hoped.

We waited for reports from the returning ships' mission, anxious to hear if Jerry was weakening. This was not to be. Thirty-nine aircraft took off with 390 men. Of those, three ships failed to return. Twelve men were killed and sixteen men parachuted and were still missing. Of the ships that returned, two more men were killed by flak and six others were wounded. Thirty-six casualties in all. Like I said, awful.

We all hoped the war was winding down. We were told just a couple of weeks ago that with Merseburg destroyed, we should just about be done with this damn war. Now no one knew for sure when any of us would be headed home and to top it all, we just learned our mission quota had been increased to thirty-five.

Going around again on a mission proved suicide for this B-24.
Photo courtesy of the National Archives.

Some planes had to dive to extinguish engine fires. Tex was one of the
best pilots ever at this. Photo courtesy of the National Archives.

On this mission Pilot Thomas O'Donnell flew just to our right
in formation. Photo courtesy of the National Archives.

JANUARY 20, 1945

Mission #22

Destination: Mannheim

Target: Railroad Bridge

My twentieth and twenty-first missions to railroad yards at Ingolstadt and Paderborn, Germany, pleasantly surprised all of us. Two more "milk runs."

Mission #22: back to Mannheim and a railroad bridge. The 301st mission for the entire group suddenly didn't seem so far away. Donovan was sick that day and we were flying with a togglier by the name of Dittman. He seemed pretty young to Tex and me, *but hell, give him a few more missions and he'll look the same as the rest of us. War has a way of aging a fellow—fast!*

"Pilot to bombardier, keep a close eye on the lead ship. Make sure our drop is good," ordered Tex. "Let's shove those bombs right down their damn Jerry throats."

"Yes sir, target in sight, sir." Dittman answered.

"Lieutenant Holmes, this is the radio operator. Reports of bad weather on our return, sir."

"Eddie, make sure you get that report," Holmes told me.

"Bombs away. Bomb bay doors closing," Dittman announced.

Heading back home was easy until we reached the French mainland. Snow was falling and headwinds were picking up. I checked my instruments and determined our ground speed was only 120 knots.

"Tex, we're a little slow getting back because of these damn headwinds. How is the fuel?"

"We should be OK," was the answer, but by the time we saw England the snow was raging and the winds had really increased.

"Tex, take heading three four zero, we should be about forty-five minutes to base," I said.

All was quiet for the next few minutes, then Tex said, "We gotta be close. Eddie, check our position."

The airfield should have been no more than eight miles ahead and I conveyed as much to Tex. The visibility, no more than a few hundred yards, and flying in this soup made all of us pretty nervous.

Just then we heard a sputtering noise. Tex blurted out, "Number four engine is gone! Check fuel, feather prop! Eddie, are you sure of our position?"

"Yes sir, we should be over Molesworth by now," I responded.

"Number four feathered," Haynes told Tex. "I don't know how long the others will last but I guess we'll find out."

"Our position is right, sir," I said again.

"There goes number two!" Haynes shouted.

"Sir, start doing S turns, we should be home by now." I said to Tex, while wondering if I had made a mistake. I re-checked my previous calculations and did so in a hurry. *No time to waste. Yes, everything checks out. Now check the instruments. Yes, all are functioning normal. Did I make a mistake? Where did I go wrong? What did I miss? Start re-checking!*

"There it is at two o'clock!" shouted our new man, Dittman. "There's Molesworth."

What a relief, I thought.

"Number three is going! Number three is going!" shouted Haynes. Just at that moment we felt the bump and heard the screeching of the tires hitting the pavement. The snow was coming down as if there was no tomorrow. We could not see far enough to spit. Before rolling 100 yards our number one engine also quit. *My God,* I thought. *That was close—too damn close.*

Bomb bay doors open.
"Let's shove those bombs right down their damn Jerry throats."
Photo courtesy of the National Archives.

JANUARY 22, 1945

Mission #23

Destination: Sterkrade

Target: Synthetic Oil Plant

Your target for today, gentlemen, is the oil plant at Sterkrade, Germany. We'll be sending up twenty-six crews. We don't expect many enemy fighters but we do expect a lot of flak. Be careful, boys, and hopefully, we can all go home soon," the briefing officer told us.

A lot of flak, what the hell did he think we were flying through all those other missions, cotton candy? Damn, if he could fly just once, maybe then he would know the meaning of the word, "careful."

I was slated to fly with another crew today aboard the ship *Daddy's Delight* because their navigator was ill. I didn't like changing crews. Bad luck. Bad luck because of a number of things: I didn't know how these new fellows would react to flak or enemy fighters, even after being given direct orders. I didn't know their voices, their weaknesses or strengths and I didn't know if any of them were ready to go over the edge. With my crew I could tell who said what to whom and what was going on without having to guess or ask. It was bad enough fighting the Krauts without having to put up with on-the-job training. It's like being on a football team. You practice with the same guys every day. You know your assignment and your buddies know theirs. All efforts are coordinated precisely, in a collective effort. You know what they're going to do on each play and vice versa. It's like that on a B-17 with your regular crew; only the game at 25,000 feet is for keeps.

We had a short delay because of weather. A good opportunity to answer a couple of letters.

January 22, 1945

My Darling,

I got about four letters from you today, and I was glad to get them. It seems that all of them pile up for about three weeks, then I get them all at once.

No, Honey, I didn't have such a Merry Christmas this year, or a happy New Year. I spent Christmas Eve from 11:30 P.M. to 4:30 A.M. in a freezing truck on icy roads going to another field to fly that morning, (Christmas Day), to Germany. That night I rode back in the truck and got in just in time to go on another raid. I was frostbitten all over. It's the coldest and hungriest I've ever been. But by now I'm used to that sort of thing. It wasn't too bad. Someone has to do this mess, it might as well be me. I'm lucky I'm still able to do anything.

It won't be long now before I'm through over here. A couple of months I guess. I'll be glad to get back there and see America. It's a lot different from these other countries.

They say that if we live to finish this tour, we go home for three weeks, then go to the Pacific. Christ, I hope not. Not for a while anyway. I'd like to come home for a few months not a few weeks.

We'll see later though whether we can be together or not.

I have not received anything from home such as packages. I don't really expect anything that causes too much trouble. And Darling, I haven't been able to get anywhere to get you anything. I'll do it as soon as possible. It seems like I say the same thing every Christmas, but I swear I can't get anywhere to even send you the money to buy something yourself. I'm going to try again tomorrow, but I'll probably be over Germany instead, as usual.

Darling, I wish the war would end, I miss you so much. I want to come back home and do as I used to. I want to be young, as I really am. I hate to worry, or have such responsibilities of an older man's life. I'm tired.

All my love always,
Edward

"Lieutenant Albertson, got time for a cup of coffee?" our pilot, Fravel, asked.

"In a minute, I want to send a letter to my folks," I said, staring outside to get a look at the weather. "Clearing up yet?"

"You've got time. I'll let you know," was his response.

January 22, 1945

Dear Dad,

Got another letter today from you. The more mail I get the better. Keep it up. Haven't gotten any mail yet as to packages. Probably be here about a week.

Well, I'm coming along pretty well now here. Things are rolling, as I like to see them roll. Expect to be home about May 1st at the latest. That is, if I get there at all.

What do you think about Betty June and I marrying after I get home and pay my debts and save about $500. Say what you think. I'm too young to know. I would like to bring her home though. We've been going together about five years this March, every day and night.

Well, send the boxes, congratulate Bill and Betty Ann for me. See you about May, I hope.

Love to all.

Your Flak Happy Son,

Edward.

"Hey Lieutenant! It's time to get rolling!" Fravel yelled.

We were flying as the "tail-end Charlie"; the last plane in the formation. But on this flight our "little friends" kept the Germans away.

It was good flying weather for us as the undercast kept the guns from getting too close. I guess we were about fifty miles or so from the target when the friendly clouds ended. "Oh my God!" our new togglier, Roberts said. "Is that flak normal?"

"Get suited up boys, looks like our luck ran out with these clouds," the pilot ordered.

Roberts seemed to fly into his flak suit. He had his gear on in record time! I would have laughed out loud if I hadn't known what was coming.

We were flying as "tail-end Charlie"—the last plane in the squadron formation. Photo courtesy of the National Archives.

"The flak looks pretty heavy, fellas; Jerry is getting zeroed in! Stay on your toes and concentrate!" Fravel said, trying to be reassuring but I could see the clouds and I didn't want to go through another episode like the one over Bonn. *Let's just get the bombs out and get the hell home!*

"Sir! A ship is going down behind us, sir!" Belcher, our top turret gunner said. "Jesus Christ! The whole wing was blown off!"

"Roberts, we're over the target, watch the lead ship," Fravel announced. We were just moments from those sweet words, "bombs away," and turning for home.

"Sir, there goes another plane," Belcher said. "Looks like one from the same squad. They must really have our range."

"Ball turret to pilot, the ship that had its wing blown off just exploded! I see two, no three chutes. How did they get out of that?"

"Bombs away!" shouted Roberts. "Closing bomb bay doors."

I moved up to pat Roberts on the shoulder and to see if our drop hit the target. "Looks like they're hitting the spot," I reported to Fravel while leaning forward spread-eagle with my hands bracing me against the bubble.

Flak was pinging the hell out of our ship. *Better get back to my position,* I thought, when all of a sudden I heard a loud swoosh. *What the hell was that? Where was this rush of air coming from?* I looked around and saw my equipment scattered everywhere. Then I noticed a shell hole just between my legs. I looked up and saw another hole through the top of the nose.

"Jesus Christ!" I shouted. "What the hell!

"What is it?" the pilot said.

"Jesus Christ!" I repeated. "An eighty-eight just went through the nose and nearly took my ass off!"

"You OK?" he asked.

I couldn't speak for a minute. That was close! I could have been split in half! "Yes sir," I finally gulped, "but that was damn close."

Maybe I had a little luck with me at that moment, I don't know. But that really scared the hell out of me when I realized what happened.

I quickly gathered my maps and pencils and started my calculations for home. "Sir, take heading two three zero, we'll avoid some of this flak. We only have a slight headwind which will also help." I radioed to the pilot.

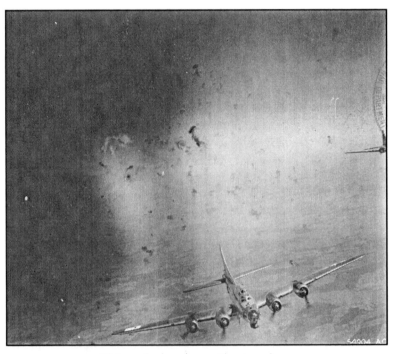
Flak explosions are getting too close.
Photo courtesy of the National Archives.

On our return we heard chatter about two planes being hit so badly that they were going to try their luck and land on the Continent. One was from the 358th and one from the 427th Squadron. And with wounded on board they could not take any extra chances of making such a long flight home.

At de-briefing we were told that a guy had nearly lost a leg, and one fellow had some shrapnel in his head. Of the twenty-six aircraft sent over, two were shot down, two were believed to have landed in Belgium and the rest had major battle damage.

"You can attest to that, can't you, Lieutenant?" Roberts said with a nod.

Boy, was he right. "Hey kid, how about buying me a beer?" I asked.

I had my beer with Roberts and introduced him to Tex and the gang. Tex was glad we made it back and drank a little more than he usually did. "No matter," he said, "the word is no flying tomorrow; the weather is too bad."

The next morning I woke up early as usual, ready to go, but found out that Tex was right again; no mission today and from the look of things we wouldn't be going up for some time. The snow was almost waist deep on the base and the winds were blowing at gale force. I re-read some mail, had a couple of smokes and tried to go back to sleep. I was tossing around until I finally said to hell with it and got up, shaved and went for some coffee and toast.

"Hey Eddie, over here!" I spotted Donovan over by one of the stoves and sat down to shoot the breeze. "I hear we're going to Berlin," he said, while sipping at his steamy cup.

"No kidding. When?"

"If the weather breaks, maybe tomorrow. It sure beats sitting around here."

The Eighth Air Force had already flown a total of ten bombing missions over the German capital prior to this, my first mission. Bombing Berlin was crucial for several reasons. First, it was after all the capital of Germany, the seat of all power of the Third Reich. Secondly, we knew that protecting Berlin was of utmost importance to the Nazi war effort, strategically as well as psychologically. This could play into our hands. Every fighter plane Jerry had in and around the capital would be in the air, which, in turn, would provide us the opportunity to destroy them. And lastly, by bombing Berlin, we could destroy or cripple the war industry in and all around the city.

The first attempt to this target by the Eighth was scheduled for March 3, 1944, but because of snowstorms and high winds the mission was cancelled. The next attempt came the next day but was recalled when snow started falling fast. Some planes never made it off the base. These were planes in the First Division. The same recall went out to the Third Division, which was well on its way to "Big B."[3]

All planes obeyed orders and returned except for one wing consisting of two 95th Group squadrons and one squadron from the 100th Group.[4] A total of twenty-nine ships made the trip. All reported that they did not receive any messages ordering their return. Headquarters knew these guys were not responding to orders and dispatched an escort of P-51s for protection. These twenty-nine ships were the first of the Eighth Air Force to drop on the German capital. Of these, five ships were lost, four from the 95th and one from the 100th. The bombing results were not immediately known because of the heavy cloud cover but it didn't much matter. What did matter was that Berlin finally was hit by the Americans. While Germany continued to lose more and more planes and pilots, America continued to add more and more planes and pilots to its arsenal.

The next raid to Berlin was two days later but the results were much different.[5] The enemy was waiting. We had dispatched 790 bombers along with 796 escort fighters for protection. About half-way to the target, the Germans noticed a gap in fighter protection and went after the 95th and 100th. After a twenty- to thirty-minute battle, these two groups lost a total of twenty-three ships and two hundred and thirty men. Two hundred and eighty men were lost or killed in two days.

---

[3] Roger Freeman, *The Mighty Eighth*, 152
[4] ibid, 113
[5] ibid, 114

This ship (the *Wee Willie* of the 91st Bomb Group) was shot down over
Oranienburg, Germany, on a mission to destroy an ordnance depot on
April 8, 1944. Some say an enemy fighter shot off the wing;
some say flak. I say who gives a damn how it was hit.
The fact is that only a few of the crew managed to parachute to safety.
Photo courtesy of the National Archives.

FEBRUARY 3, 1945

Mission #25

Destination: Berlin

Target: Multiple Military Objectives

After a January 22 mission to Sterkrade, the group stood down for over a week. On February 1, we revisited Mannhein and bombed its railroad yards. On this run, however, unlike the previous one, we suffered no planes lost nor casualties. We were part of 937 bombers that flew that day.

This was the Bomb Group's 311th mission and the eleventh raid to Berlin, but my first. I was assigned not to Tex's ship but to Lt. Darwin Knudson's ship. The lieutenant was a fine pilot and good soldier, but as I've said I didn't like changing crews. It seemed like nearly every time I did, that plane and crew got it on a later mission. I felt like my time was coming or rather, like I was being chased by time. I didn't know which but I didn't like it.

Leading the 303rd for this mission was former Deputy Commanding Officer and the acting CO, Lt. Col. Lewis Lyle. We had all thirty-nine planes participating on this raid.

While running through our pre-flight check, our pilot announced he was having some problems with one of the engines. The blades were turning but he could not get the RPMs needed.

"Pilot to crew, there's a problem in number four engine, we can't get enough manifold pressure. We'll have a delay until the ground crew can fix it. Stand down until further notice."

Damn, I thought, *this is not the way to start a mission.*

The ground crew started working on the problem right away as the rest of us gathered inside the tent and took advantage of the warmth and the freshly brewed coffee. Not knowing how long we would be delayed, a couple of the crew lay down to grab some needed shuteye.

I hoped this wouldn't take long. I'd rather be up there flying than down here waiting. Within a few minutes a mechanic opened the tent flap and said the problem had been found and should be fixed in thirty to forty minutes. *This shouldn't be too bad,* I thought. *We can tag on to another group and get our mission completed. One mission closer to going home.*

Within an hour we were up and beginning to catch up to the nearest group ahead. I couldn't tell who we were flying with because none of us could distinguish any of their tail insignia. Anyway, we were going to finish our mission.

A few clouds were around but no Jerry fighters to speak of. However the flak was starting to zero in on our group.

"They just hit the lead flight!" one of the crew shouted.

I looked out the bubble and saw the lead plane on fire. The fire was spreading fast and I wondered out loud, "Why don't you bail out!?"

Yet the plane continued on the bomb run! The fire was spreading directly under the plane and it wouldn't be long before the bomb bay would be ablaze. The lead ship dropped its bombs and I then heard our bombardier announce bombs away. *Son-of-a-bitch,* I thought, *that pilot stayed on his bomb run while on fire and completed his mission.* That took guts, real guts.

After the drop, the ship pulled away from the formation, still ablaze. Some chutes were seen but the count was not clear. Suddenly there was a bright explosion and the plane disappeared, leaving nothing but small fireballs and dark smoke filling the sky, replacing what was just a second ago ten American flyboys.

We turned to follow the group back home.

It wasn't long before I heard the tail gunner announce, "Sir, enemy fighters going after the group behind us."

Not much was said for a moment or two when suddenly I heard the tail gunner shout, "Sir! Enemy planes heading our way, they bypassed the last group and are attacking our rear ships!"

I leaned over and looked out my side window, wondering what the hell he was talking about. "Jesus Christ! There must be two or three hundred planes out there and they're coming after us!"

"Call out those fighters and don't shout over the intercom." The pilot ordered.

"Two coming in at two o'clock, there's another one at six o'clock!"

The pilot stayed on his bomb run while on fire. That took guts, real guts.
Photo courtesy of the National Archives.

This is one of the unlucky ones. This is the beginning of her death dive. Photo courtesy of the National Archives.

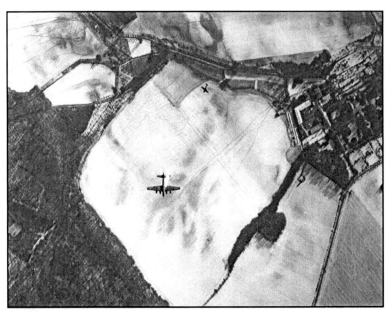

This German FW 190 shot down the B-17 pictured. After hitting her, the enemy pilot followed her to the ground to make sure of her death. Photo courtesy of the National Archives.

We were firing at everything! I was sure we would be goners but a few moments later our pilot directed the ship into some cloud cover and lost the fighters. They would be searching for us; we all knew that. I just couldn't figure out why we were attacked and not the group behind us. We kept our guard up but didn't see any more enemy fighters.

The chatter on the intercom was of Jerry seeing our planes stretching over three hundred miles. I could not imagine what that looked like from the ground. Jerry must have seen miles of contrails knowing somewhere in his country an armada of planes was wreaking havoc on the Fatherland.

On our return we broke off at the Zuider Zee, an inlet of seventy-five to eighty miles long from the North Sea in Holland, and made a beeline for Molesworth. At our de-briefing our lieutenant informed us we had joined up with the "Bloody 100th."

"Jesus Christ. No wonder," the pilot said as he shook his head and walked out the door.

Everyone was aware of what happened to the 100th during a raid to Regensburg a year ago.

The 100th was tail-end Charlie that day, the favored segment of a formation which was vulnerable to attack. Three planes had gone down in their low squadron; three out of six. Others were shot down as well. Out of their total of twenty-two planes dispatched that day, nine were shot down. Nearly half.

But the reason the German fighters went after the 100th was because one of their ships that day, piloted by Captain Knox, had lowered its wheels to the German Luftwaffe, signaling their intent to surrender. The plane had already lost two engines and was losing speed. As a lame duck and a sitting duck, he didn't want to be shot down while defenseless.

The wheels down, a universal sign of surrender, lured the Germans in close so they could escort the crippled ship to one of their air bases. Once the fighters came along side, the B-17 gunners blew the escorting enemy fighters out of the sky. His wheels went up and Captain Knox made a run for home.

Within minutes other enemy fighters swooped down on Knox's ship and he too was blasted out of the sky.

Ever since that first deception, the Luftwaffe would identify and single out the 100th. They would pass and ignore other bomber groups in a total effort to wipe out that entire group. And at times, they came damn close to doing it. This violation of the "Code of the Air," was as revolting to the Germans as the murder of American prisoners at Malmedy was to us. Certain codes should not be broken, even in "all's fair in love and war" disposition.[6]

Later we were told that there was only one wounded crewmember in our group. Amazing. This was my twenty-fifth mission with ten to go. It was also my second mission with Lieutenant Knudson and although we returned safe, I still didn't like the changes. After dinner I wrote home.

February 3, 1945

Dear Dad,

Haven't heard from you for sometime. What's up?

Been pretty rough here lately but seems to be clearing a little, and the work goes on as usual.

I ran into a boy from Maury yesterday. His name is Cole. His sister taught sewing at Granby.

So the brother turned patriotic again and took off from the states. He should know when his lucks up and sit tight at home. I'll get boy scouts to help me cross the streets when I get back home. My luck's about all shot. I can't have any more.

I'll be waiting for some boxes and some letters. Tell Ena Taylor to write. So, our star quarterback, is still at home. And he was out of high school a year and a half before I was. Keep up the morale at the home front.

Your son,

Edward

It was February 8 and five days since our last mission. The only missions we executed in the past few days were of fuel heists from other quarters to stay warm, and trips to our trash dump to get rid of the dead rats we killed after we caught them stealing our food. *Hell, yesterday I saw a fellow cut away bite marks on his apple before he*

---

[6] Edward Jablonski, *Flying Fortress: The Illustrated Biography of the B-17s and the Men Who Flew Them* (New York: Doubleday and Company, Inc., 1965), 178-180

could eat it. I'm glad for one thing: I'm not in some damn frozen foxhole with Jerry lobbing artillery shells at me.

I read some mail from my girl. I felt there was some trouble back home, with her, with us, but I couldn't put my finger on it. *The best thing I can do is write her and find out what is the trouble.*

February 8, 1945

My Darling,

Today I got a letter from you and you said that you were worried about me. I won't tell you that there is no need to worry, because there is. But don't you do the worrying. Let me do it. I'm fighting to come back. I know I've got to, to get you. You are the reason I've got to get back. I've got to. I will.

You said you would not marry me on my return. I cannot discuss it now. I don't know enough about it. I don't know if I want to or not as soon as I get home. I don't know if I'll be mad or not if you don't.

I need time to straighten myself out. I've got to get away from this mess and think, think so much I'll know what I'm doing is what I should do. I don't understand this life I'm leading. The things I'm doing I don't understand. I know I have to, yet I shouldn't, but still I should.

My mind is like a crazy person's, all mixed up. Drinking doesn't help, sleeping doesn't help. Time should straighten me up.

Just keep yourself pure and clean, have hope in my being, pray for us both every day and night. Wait for me Darling, I'll be back. I need you terribly.

I love you,
Edward

Our boys were giving the Germans hell and Patton was pushing. We knew we had to keep flying to destroy railroads, oil fields and other lines of supply. We would stop this mad Hitler machine and take his dream and shove it down his damn Nazi throat.

This is a picture taken during my first raid to Berlin on February 3, 1945.
The smoke below is from fires started in the Templehof area that
blanketed part of the capital. This raid had over 1000 planes taking part.
Our ships were still approaching Berlin as many groups were heading
home. The sight was awesome and so were the chances of returning
bombers colliding with other ships heading to the target.
Photo courtesy of the National Archives.

Lead crew, 359th Bomb Squadron. Mission: Lutzkendorf, February 9, 1945. Photo courtesy of the 303rd Bomb Group Association and the National Archives.

FEBRUARY 9, 1945

Mission #26

Destination: Lutzkendorf

Target: Oil Plant

Your mission today, gentlemen, is the oil plant at Lutzkendorf, Germany. This is an eight-hour mission and we will put up all thirty-nine aircraft. The secondary target is the railway center at Erfurt. Bombing will be visual. Good luck, gentlemen. Let's give our boys on the ground extra help today," the briefing officer said, then dropped his smoke, stamped it cold, and turned to exit, signaling us to get moving.

Approaching the target, I was glad we had nearly two hundred P-51s as escorts. As the lead plane in our squadron I was especially glad to have them along. I was again flying with a new crew, piloted by Lt. Cecil Gates whom I had just met at the briefing. Lieutenant Webber was the bombardier and seemed, along with the pilot, like a pretty square fellow.

"Eight minutes to the bomb run, sir," I told Gates. "We're on time and right on course."

"Roger; flak ahead boys, flak suits on, look sharp, it's starting to look thick! Bombardier, I'm turning on the autopilot, you're flying the plane. We're two minutes, thirty seconds to bomb run."

Bamm! Bamm! The bursts were everywhere. We were bouncing all over the place, unpredictably, like a bouncing football on the field of play! All I could think of was another German eighty-eight coming through the compartment, only this time hitting its intended target. Webber was calm but bouncing all over. BAMM! Bits of flak were tearing up my flight suit! This was too close for me. Another piece, right through the sole of my boot! "Let's get the hell out of here!" someone yelled.

"Sir, two ships from the low squadron just got it. Hell! One of them is torn in half!" the co-pilot said, trying to keep calm. "The other one is heading down, fast. No fire seen, maybe they can get control. My God, one chute is open. How in the hell did he get out of there?"

I didn't want to look. I was so sick of seeing my friends getting blown out of the sky. Bamm! Another explosion! Fire broke out just behind Webber, caused by some smoldering flak. I reached for my fire extinguisher and doused the flame.

"Bombs away!" shouted Webber.

I was just about to give Gates our heading when I heard the waist gunner shout, "They hit Bailey's ship!"

I jumped to my window to see for myself. I had to. My old friend Ed Bartowski, my bombardier in my original crew with Tex was assigned to that ship. Number two and number three engines were on fire!

"Jump!" I shouted. "Jump, you bastards!"

"No chutes yet. Looks like an engine has been feathered. The other engine looks like it's running wild, kind of like a tire out of balance," I heard someone say.

"They're losing altitude, sir," I announced. "They're losing power and altitude fast."

Bailey's plane was straggling too far behind and even though I knew they could get the ship under control, until then, they would be sitting ducks for the Hun.

"Damn, I hope he makes it," Gates said. "Now give me a heading and man your weapon."

"There goes Mauger's ship," someone said.

Jesus, I thought. Ships on either side of us were gone and two more ships from the low squadron were also lost.

This was my twenty-sixth mission and even though Jerry had been taking a beating I knew this war wasn't over, and any luck I might have left seemed to be drying up. *Nine more missions to go. Lord, I hope I make it.*

At de-briefing we were told Bailey's plane was last seen heading north and Lieutenant Mauger's plane made it to a friendly field. All of his crew were safe. I asked one of the officers to let me know if any word came in later about Bartowski. The total of known dead from the mission was thirteen. One was wounded in action but returned to base. The number missing was also thirteen; thirteen, the unluckiest number of all. I headed back to the barracks for some rest. This damn war was really beginning to get to me and I needed some time to think. Time to think about anything, except nine more missions.

Lieutenant Bailey's ship went in. Bartkowski was aboard.
He replaced the tail gunner pictured here, bottom, fourth from left.
As it turned out, one man's luck was the other's nightmare.
Photo courtesy of the National Archives.

When I opened the door to my barracks, Tex was sitting on the edge of his bunk, just staring, quietly staring at the floor.

"Tex, how are ya? How was your mission?" I asked almost in a mumble.

"I heard Bartowski is missing. Any word on his ship? Ah, yeah, the mission was OK, the usual mess. What do you know about Bart?" was his humble reply.

I turned and made my way to Bart's footlocker, knowing we had to go through it and throw anything out that may embarrass his family or girl. I had lost friends before but none like Bartowski.

"He was in Lieutenant Bailey's bird. I watched as they lost two engines. Bailey was able to feather both before they fell low and behind. We lost radio contact immediately, and soon visual. I'm sure they got it; enemy fighters were lagging behind them, away from the formation.

"Tex, help me clear out his footlocker before some private comes in and mails it all to his family," I added.

Tex and I spent little time doing the necessary deed. Upon completion, Tex looked me up and down. "What the hell happened? Look at your flight suit, Eddie."

Looking down I noticed for the first time the raggedy condition it was in. "Flak hit us pretty good, I guess I had some close calls. I didn't give it much notice at the time. It was only after we taxied and shut down the engines that we started counting the number of flak holes in the nose. We quit after two hundred. I think we were lucky today."

There were a few minutes of silence before Tex spoke up. "Eddie, it looks like the weather is going to have us socked in for a few days. Some of the guys were thinking about asking for a little time off. You know some R&R. There's this old mansion not too far from here run by the Red Cross, just for us flyboys. We can play some golf, swim, or do nothing but eat ourselves to death. What do you say?"

Pondering his question but quickly realizing the weather was probably the same all over southern England, I said, "Nope, no thanks, I have nine more missions and the sooner I get done the sooner I can go home. You guys go ahead, I'm staying here."

"Who? Not me, Eddie." Tex replied "I only asked because I thought you could use some rest. I'm with you, buddy; let's finish up and get the hell back home."

The weather had us socked in for six days. I had all the rest I needed. I was ready to get back and finish this tour. To hell with luck and to hell with dying.

Ships on either side of us were going down.
Nine more missions to go—I hope I make it.
Photo courtesy of the National Archives.

FEBRUARY 15, 1945

Mission #27

Destination: Dresden

Target: Military Objectives

As early morning broke over the horizon, we found ourselves on our way to bomb Dresden. We were a little worried because of the losses of the February 3 raid there, one raid I was glad not to be a part of.

As we all knew, Dresden was a largely populated area with thousands of refugees. Reconnaissance pictures had shown huddled masses sleeping in the streets. We were aware also that there were thousands sleeping in what was left of the buildings. We knew with the bombing of military targets in and around the city that more civilians would be killed including old men, women and children. None of us wanted to think about that but we did our duty, remembering that the Germans bombed London, Portsmouth, and other civilian towns and cities, killing thousands of English men, women and children. We had to do what the great Union general, William Tecumseh Sherman (in the American Civil War), did on his "March to the Sea" campaign in 1864. His army literally destroyed everything in its path. Sherman would make sure that every soldier, non-soldier, woman and child would be so sick of war that they would lose the will to fight.

We were all still incensed about the eighty-six American soldiers murdered after being taken prisoner at Malmedy on December 17 during the beginning of the Battle of the Bulge. The massacre of our boys, after surrendering and being taken prisoner, was still fresh on our minds. A thing like that doesn't fade easily from your memory.

At Malmedy, some Jerry officer named Peiper and his Panzer Battalion had taken an American truck convoy by surprise and shot them up pretty bad. As he continued to advance, this Kraut commander ordered his foot soldiers following his tanks to round up the Americans and keep them as prisoners. It took a couple of hours to assemble the captured and wounded men. Then the Germans lined them up and cut them down by machine-gun fire. The cowards who did this, walked among the dead to make sure anyone with a breath left in his body got a pistol shot to the head.[7]

Again I found myself flying with a new crew; Lt. Clem Rogers. He seemed like a swell fella. While loading our gear I asked the togglier, Wilson, "Hey Wilson, if I get hit by shrapnel in the leg, what's the first thing you do?"

Wilson looked at me with a smart-ass stare and said, "Don't worry, Lieutenant, I know my business."

"Hey! Wait a minute! I said what are you going to do if I get hit? If my life is in your hands, I want to make damn sure you know what to do. Now, what are you going to do if I get hit?"

Wilson straightened up and answered, "OK, first I'll check your oxygen, then I'll…"

I stopped him in mid-sentence since I could tell he knew. "OK, OK. I'm getting close to my thirty-fifth mission and I just want to make sure what kind of man I'm flying with."

The takeoff that day was a mess. Visibility was near zero. Our radio operator announced that one plane had already gone down about three or four hundred yards west of the east-west runway and was burning. I bet he hit those electric cables. I couldn't see any smoke. Hell, we would have been lucky to see even a hundred yards in that miserable weather. The one good thing about the lousy weather was that there wouldn't be enemy fighters and it could also provide us cover against that deadly flak. *First things first,* I thought. *We still need to get off the ground. Holmes and Haynes weren't flying today. Those lucky bastards.*

I can't remember how many times Dresden was attacked, but it was an old city filled with medieval architecture and works of fine art, or used to be. Few buildings were left standing by 1945. However, we still needed to take out any remaining industry and if destroying these cities would whip the Germans, I was all for it. They didn't worry about London after their V-1 and V-2 rockets had obliterated everything, including thousands and thousands of innocent civilians.

The mission went well. After we dropped, the pilot decided to take us down to treetop level to look for targets of opportunity to

---

[7] James M. Gavin, *On to Berlin: Battles of an Airborne Commander, 1943-1946* (New York: Viking Press, 1978), 213

strafe. We had plenty of fuel left that day because we had a hundred-mile-an-hour tail wind on the way to the target, which had subsided before heading back. I put my flak suit back on as we approached five thousand feet. We could get some small arms fire flying that low but we had a chance to knock out some of those God damn eighty-eights and maybe a few Krauts with them.

"OK boys, we're heading down to about two hundred feet. Keep a lookout for flak batteries and anything else you think we should hit," Rogers said.

At two hundred feet and flying over two hundred miles an hour, even I marveled at what a weapon we had: this great Flying Fortress with thirteen fifty-caliber machine guns. Now this was flying!

"Open farmland ahead, boys," Wilson said.

I was looking out the bubble when I noticed a row of haystacks ahead. Haystacks as big as barns. As we approached I could not believe what I was seeing. These haystacks were collapsing! It wasn't that windy and I wondered, *What the hell?*

Wilson yelled, "Up! Up! Up!"

Ahead I saw this huge haystack fall away, revealing the biggest eighty-eight I had ever seen! This mammoth gun was staring me right in the eye! *My God*, I thought. *He can't miss!* An orange flash came from the barrel as I blinked; I thought I was a goner. I didn't know how, but he missed. I caught my breath and started shooting my fifty-cal at every damn haystack in every field. I only stopped when we were far enough away to breathe normally.

"If that's not enough to scare you to hell I don't know what is," I said to no one in particular. Wiping his brow, Wilson turned my way and gave me the thumbs up.

"Navigator, reports from Group Leader, some planes are running out of fuel and having to ditch in the Channel. We should have plenty of fuel but check your instruments. How do we look?"

"OK sir, I could hear chatter over the radio about headwinds being pretty bad. A storm front is heading southward. We are heading north of the front. Keep present course. I'll re-check every few minutes for changes and make adjustments," I answered.

Some minutes later I called the pilot to report we were seventy-five miles west of Great Yarmouth and should avoid all the headwinds hitting the other ships.

"Crew, take a look down there. I've counted seven planes already in the Channel. I've radioed ahead and asked for air-sea rescue," Rogers announced. "Looks like we have plenty of fuel with some to spare. We'll need it; Molesworth is getting snowed in with visibility down to near zero. We may have to head to another base."

"Sir, take heading two six zero," I said a few minutes later. "That course should head us straight in to base."

Our landing went smoothly even though a number of other ships had a tough time. I saw one ship come in with wheels up and only one engine. They made it OK. I knew that crew was relieved.

"Lieutenant! Lieutenant!" Rogers called to me outside the briefing room.

"Yes sir."

"Lieutenant Albertson, that was some damn good navigating today. How did you know the wind speed when we didn't have any reports telling us?"

"Ah, that's a navigator's secret sir," I answered.

He simply smiled and turned to enter the de-briefing hut, still puzzled. Some would call it luck; I would call it experience. Well, experience with maybe a little luck. I was lucky enough to catch a glimpse of the direction of waves through the cloud cover using Wilson's bombsite, and calculated the wind speed. Anyway, it was a navigator's secret; still is.

Thinking of the crews of those seven ships that ditched, I couldn't help but wonder what happened to the seventy men. We all knew the story of T/Sgt Forrest Vosler. His ship had to ditch during a raid over Bremen in December 1943.

Vosler, from Livonia, New York, was the radioman of his doomed B-17 when he was wounded in both legs and thighs by twenty-mm cannon fire from swooping German fighters. He was able to brace himself up against his table and continued to fight when another shell burst nearby, sending splinters into his chest, face and eyes. He was falling in and out of consciousness, nearly blinded but somehow managed to continue firing his weapon at the blurry shapes coming at his ship. Knowing his plane would have to ditch, soon, by touch alone, T/Sgt Vosler fixed his radio and sent out SOS signals for air-sea rescue. After his plane ditched in the Channel he felt for one of his buddies; finding, grabbing, pulling and holding his badly wounded body until others could help them both into a small raft. He spent nearly ten months in hospitals after that. Being blinded was bad enough but doing such a thing in freezing cold water was pure bravery. Sergeant Vosler was flying on the "Jersey Bounce Jr." and for his heroism he received the Medal of Honor.[8]

I had a couple drinks after chow and wrote home. I had received a letter from Dad telling me Doug, my older brother, had been wounded in action in the Pacific and was in the hospital. He didn't say too much else except that Doug was trading hand grenades with some Jap. My brother killed the Jap but the Jap got my brother too. He was hit with shrapnel in his back and legs when the Jap hand grenade bounced off a rock and exploded above him. My father said he would be OK. Doug was always a tough kid. He volunteered right after Pearl Harbor becoming a scout/sniper in the First Marine division. I hoped Dad was right.

Well anyway I had just flown my twenty-seventh mission. I was ready to be done with this business and return home.

---

[8] Freeman, *The Mighty Eighth,* 102, 269

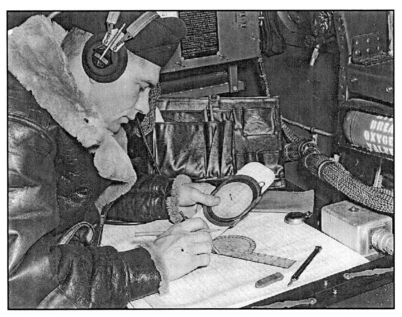

This is where I do my calculations when I'm not firing at enemy fighters.
Photo courtesy of the National Archives.

This is a raid to the city of Dresden on April 17, 1945.
It was during the February 15 raid to the city that we decided to fly at
treetop level to do some strafing of our own. This is where we learned
first hand how haystacks could fall apart and we would
come face to face with those infamous German 88mm cannons.
Photo courtesy of the National Archives.

"Hell's Angels" lost twenty-three aircraft to ditching. There were hundreds of others lost by other groups. These fellows were lucky. Many died upon impact or from exposure to freezing seas. Some only lasted for a few minutes.
Photo courtesy of the National Archives.

This is the ship that Technical Sergeant Forrest Vosler (Medal of Honor recipient) was assigned to before it was forced to ditch. Note the hole blown through the nose just above the name "Jersey Bounce." This is about the same size hole left in the nose of the plane I was flying in on the February 23 raid to Sterkrade, Germany when I nearly got cut in half. Photo courtesy of the National Archives.

FEBRUARY 16, 1945

Mission #28

Destination: Langerdreer

Target: Synthetic Oil Fields

Good morning, gentlemen, your mission for today is a synthetic oil field at Langerdreer. The secondary target is Munster. Before I go any further I want you to know that your mission results from yesterday have led us to declare Dresden a dead city."

Cheers went up for a moment, then quickly died out. We had no wish to risk any more crews over that place. Jerry had to be ready for a break; we were taking him out. And the boys on the ground who had done such a good job at Bastogne, were now on the outskirts of Haguenau, France, ready to start their move into Germany. Yes, we thought and believed, Germany was on the retreat.

I was assigned to Lieutenant Bixby's ship. Another change I didn't like. I went to the commanding officer with fire in my eyes. "Why am I assigned to another plane? I know their navigator is well and is lying about his illness."

"You will do as you are ordered, Lieutenant!" the major shot back. "Now get to your assignment or face a court-martial."

I glared straight at the major and blasted back, "He is no more sick than I am. He is nothing but a God damned coward."

"That's enough, Lieutenant! Now do as you are ordered and get into the air!"

"Yes sir. I'll go this time but if that bastard pulls this again I swear I'll..."

"You'll do nothing, Lieutenant, except follow orders. Now get out of my office and out of my sight."

I went to Bixby's plane and found that the only person I knew was the young bombardier, Roberts. "How are you Eddie, uh, Lieutenant? Nice to be flying with you again."

There was yet another change that morning. Bixby's usual co-pilot was assigned to another plane and he had a new one assigned to his crew—fresh from training.

I acknowledged Roberts with a nod, stowed my gear and got ready for God only knew what. My luck maybe was up. I could feel my surroundings closing in.

We didn't see much enemy fighter action and it was a good thing as it turned out, because I didn't see any of our supposed thirty-eight P-51 escort fighters around either. I'm sure they were flying down low, giving the Germans hell. Flak was pretty bad for some of us but only one plane was shot down.

Sighting good ol' Molesworth in the distance, as always, we were pretty happy and relieved to be nearly home.

As we made our turn to final approach I knew we were banking at too much of an angle. I looked at the bombardier Roberts just as he shouted, "What the hell is going on?"

The plane was turning too sharply, an impossible seventy to eighty degrees!

I grabbed my chair and stuck one leg against the bulkhead, bracing for the worst. *Christ*, I thought, *after all this, I'm going to die while landing after a successful mission!*

At that moment I heard the engines put to full power and the pilot yell, "I've got it! I'm taking over!"

The whole ship was jerking, metal squealing; I just knew it was about to break apart under the strain. The pilot let out a loud groan and pulled us out of what was sure death. We were only a few yards off the ground when we bounced hard on the runway with the engines at nearly full power.

"Brace yourselves boys! We're going to use up all the pavement today!" Bixby shouted.

I turned and saw the pavement getting shorter and shorter. We were going too damn fast and I thought we would go in nose first at the end of the runway.

"Hell, hold on!" I shouted to Roberts. We slowed just as we were running out of concrete, quickly turned and slid onto the grassy area. I took a breath or two and thought, *Jesus, Bixby just saved our ass!*

As I exited I turned to the co-pilot and instantly realized he was the S-O-B bringing us in too steep and nearly killing us all! I grabbed him with my left hand and turned him to face me while reaching in my jacket and pulling out my forty-five with my right. With two clicks of my weapon, I chambered a bullet and pushed the gun into his neck saying, "If you ever take a chance with my life again Lieutenant, I'll blow your God-damn head off, you son-of-a-bitch!"

No one said a word—no one—not one word. I wasn't the only one close to killing this cocky-ass co-pilot.

I made my way back to my barracks and tried to cool off. After dinner and a few smokes I thought to write home. No one over here ever knows when his time is up. That son-of-a-bitch.

                                        February 16, 1945
    Dear Dad,
    I hope to be finished here soon and maybe home in a couple of months. Things are still pretty rough but I can see the end. I've been reading in the *Stars and Stripes* about news back home. It doesn't all sound to good. What gives? Write me and let me know and don't forget the cigarettes.

    Love to all,
    Your son,
    Edward

Crew of lead ship, 359th Bomb Squadron.
Mission: Gelsenkirchen, February 19, 1945. Pilot: Captain G. R. Sirany.
Photo courtesy of the 303rd Bomb Group Association
and the National Archives.

FEBRUARY 19, 1945

Mission #29

Destination: Gelsenkirchen

Target: Coking Plant

We broke through some low level clouds to find a beautiful deep blue sky on the journey to the target. Blue and peaceful so high above all the strife; desperation and death below. I had to fight the urge to just sit back and watch this serene morning lengthen into day. We had some one hundred of our little friends along for comfort. For a change we left no contrails telegraphing our presence, due to the lack of humidity in the air.

It dawned upon me that a better situation might never present itself to once and for all destroy the bridge over the Rhine River near Remagen. The whole Eighth Air Force has been trying to destroy that bridge for weeks but weather prevented a good shot at it.

"Tex!" I called, "Listen, I have a proposition for you. This weather is perfect for us to take our group down and blast that damned bridge at Remagen right off the map."

"Orders are to bomb Gelsenkirchen, Eddie. If need be we'll hit the secondary target at Munster. Taking a chance to blow that bridge is risky enough but disobeying orders, well, I don't know," Tex said back.

"Sir, the weather is perfect and I can set a course to drop right in the middle of it. This is the best chance we've had to level her. Tex, we'll be heroes! Think of the medals! We can get this done." Once more, I said, "I'll need to make a course change in less than three minutes. Think about it. This may even be our ticket home."

"I don't need three minutes Eddie," Tex shot back. "I want that bridge just as much as you do but we have orders. We best carry them out. Maybe next time."

Tex was one who followed orders to the tee. I was too but this was different. I could route us over that bridge, take it out, then we could be heading home. Home to the States, not Molesworth.

Sometimes the weather was so beautiful I almost forgot we were in a war.
Photo courtesy of the National Archives.

Then again, maybe Tex was right. His judgment had not failed us so far. *Maybe on another mission*, I thought. *Hell, let's just finish the job any way we can.*

On our way to de-briefing after landing, we saw a ship send up a flare, signaling wounded on board.

"I wonder who it is? I thought we had a pretty easy time of it today," I mentioned to Haynes. "Any ships lost other than the one early return?"

"None that I know of, Eddie. Say, let's go lend a hand since we're already half-way to the plane. Anyone object?" Haynes asked.

Everyone else said OK. I kept my mouth shut. I had removed five legs so far and I didn't want to do it again. So far that has been the hardest thing I've done, removing body parts. I'll never get used to it. Some say when you do, you stop living. I don't want to stop living, not yet anyway.

"Lieutenant! Give me a hand here!" the medic shouted.

I turned slowly, thinking, *Oh hell, not again.* As I did I saw he was asking someone else. I noticed the sick look on this guy's face as the medic handed him a blanket. It turned out to be another waist gunner on the ship, *Sweet Rosie O'Grady.* One of Lieutenant Walder's crew.

"Hey, let's head back," I said. "They have enough help here, we'd only be in the way."

At de-briefing, a new officer was doing the reviewing and questioning. Some guys were standing around mumbling about this wise guy's attitude.

"Hello fellas, what's up?" I asked.

"You'll find out," was the answer.

This new desk-jockey started in on us as though we were on Germany's side!

"Sir," Tex interrupted, "we just got back and my men are pretty tired. Can't we lighten up some? There's not a lot to report today anyway."

This jerk looked Holmes up and down and said, "Let's see here, Lieutenant. You have flown on how many missions?"

"Twenty-nine, sir," Holmes answered raising his voice just loud enough and leaning over his desk just far enough for this new know-it-all idiot to get the picture.

The de-briefing officer paused and then said, "I believe you may have a point, Lieutenant. Next!" He shouted to the next crew awaiting de-briefing.

We didn't care too much for guys like him. And ol' Tex was fed up enough to start issuing some orders of his own.

The next morning I awoke to more snow on the ground than I had seen in a month. No word about any missions today. After shaving we headed to the mess hall to see what was going on. It looked like we would be socked in for a few days. A couple of us decided to ask for some passes to London. We received permission to go but found ourselves stuck on base. The snow had us pinned down but good, and the prospects for more over the next forty-eight hours kept even us daredevils tied to our barracks.

A few days had passed and again I was bored as hell. I don't know what was worse, the boredom or getting shot at. I think I'd rather be dodging flak, to tell the truth.

"Hey Eddie!" Tex shouted, "Here's a package for you. I was at the post office and thought I'd save you the trip."

A package from home. Thank God, smokes and a letter from Dad.

Dear Son;

We have your two letters. We are very glad to hear that you consider it a safe bet that you will be home within a few months. Probably you will. I'm sure you will be flying a few more missions before you leave that part of the world.

All are well here; Mother is fine, as are Bobby and Mary. Douglas seems to be getting over his wounds OK. I talked to Buddy Chandler the other day; he is on a patrol boat out of Norfolk, patrols along the coast.

I note what you say regarding the feeling among the people back home towards the men in the service, more especially towards the men who have actually seen fighting.

Now, son, here are the reasons for the difference between you and the people who are at home; they are simple and few:

You are back to the fundamentals of living. You are getting along with the barest of necessities; you have something to eat, something to wear, and the simplest things to amuse yourself with. You have no living to earn; you have only one thing to worry about and that is the biggest thing in the world to worry about—to stay alive. To keep from being killed by someone who is trying his level best to kill you and your friends. People at home are not on that basis.

Everything else is subordinated to doing your best to stay alive. Nothing but that counts; all of the rest of the things you have been taught in your life, beside eating and keeping yourself clean, amount to nothing, in your present situation.

In joining the Army, or the Marines or the Navy, especially to a man who goes in a combat outfit and sees fighting, a man gives up everything but his honor. He foregoes almost all forms of pleasure, companionship, and domestic life. He lives a life of the crudest form. Although he would not admit it to a soul, and although he gripes all the time about it, he really takes pride in the fact that he is able to live that kind of a life and get by in good shape, and stay alive. The man, or men, who do this are also the last in the world to admit that there is any such thing as "honor" connected with their enlistment, but it is there nevertheless.

To prove to you that "honor," as we call it, plays a large part in a man's enlistment, that man who enlists and does his best for his country has no patience with those stay-at-homes who SEEM to him to be going about their everyday work, unconcerned and apparently unconscious of the lives that men in combat outfits live.

So, boiled down, son, it is you who have changed, not us. You have seen life in its rawest, crudest form, and you have no patience with those people who still think as you did before you had your present experience.

You must also remember this, for it is important, that before you enlisted in the army, others who had gone through the same experience as you are now, felt the same way towards you and the rest of the civilians.

So it is you and your fellows who have changed. Not the people.

It is likewise true that many people here at home are unconcerned to a great extent as to how the war goes. It is also true that many people care nothing about the war except as to how much money they can make during these times. I will say this, and it is true, it is a fact, those who put themselves first are mostly foreigners, people who have come to this country to make a living. While they profess patriotism, they have it not, except for show. But the great bulk, 99.99999999% of Americans, are patriotic and feel deeply where our men are concerned.

Naturally the folks at home cannot be expected to realize what you folks are going through, in your section of the world, in Europe, China and Italy. Only first-hand experience can show them. So after the fighting is over, and you have returned, you and your friends, that is, you and the rest of the men who have seen service, will feel a kinship toward each other that nothing will dissipate and you will band yourselves together in an association, either one that you will form yourselves or one already existing. You will do this because you feel closer to each other, and you will feel apart from civilians.

This has happened to almost every ex-soldier in the history of every country, so it is natural and is accepted.

The returning veterans must not accept the everyday, commonplace, feelings of the civilian for "complacency." The civilian can do nothing about it, except to send his sons, husbands, and fathers off to war and hope they will return. He can support the war effort, buy bonds, lend his money, do without things he has had all his life, and in our case especially, and this is a phenomena of the present administration, listen periodically to the politicians tell us that we are not doing our part in the war. FOOLS!

So remember this, you have changed since you have been away. When you return you will wonder why we haven't changed with you. But in time you will take up where you left off in large part. But you will remember these days of war, and what you did, and your friends did, and probably as long as you live you will feel closer to your country than those feel who stay at home.

This is why I do not feel too sorry for those of you who have seen active service. You have paid your debt to your country, you have earned your keep. Many of us haven't had the chance.

Regarding a negotiated peace, that is as likely to happen as the sky is to fall. Only a few preachers fell for it, it was a program fostered by an Englishwoman who is half-cracked, although she is still outside of an insane asylum. Why, I don't know!

Pay no attention to such stories. They mean nothing. Germany and Japan will be destroyed as nations in so far as they are able to make war again—for a long, long time. And even if we, ourselves, were so minded, there is Russia, China, France, Greece, even Italy, and England who have some say in the matter.

It is true, today as always, that we need more people to think of the United States than of other countries, but we must not lose sight of the other countries also. What affects them will also affect us, in time. If slavery is practiced in other countries and is allowed to exist, it will only be a question of time before it is practiced here.

We don't have to worry about a thing except to see that people are free, in other countries AND IN OUR OWN.

That, my boy, is what you are fighting for.

Write us and give us the score.

Yours, DAD.

"Tex, some Luckys," as I tossed over a couple of packs, "gifts from my Dad."

"What news from home? And thanks for the smokes," responded Tex.

"Just a few words about what to expect when I get home and not to worry too much about what we read in the papers. He also thinks Germany and Japan will not be allowed to negotiate a peaceful end to war but rather will have to surrender unconditionally. Other than that not much more." I said. "I'm heading over to the club to have a few drinks, why don't you join me? With the weather like it is we'll probably be grounded for a few more days anyway."

"Yeah, maybe later," Tex replied.

I was right. The weather had us locked down for more than ten days. A day or two is OK for a rest, but a long stretch like this makes you sick of the same old stuff on base. It seems nothing ever changes.

These are bridges blown up at Cologne, Germany.
We could have done the same to the Remagen Bridge while on a bombing raid to Gelsenkirchen. This was during our February 19 mission. The weather was clear and I could have taken us straight in. Thank the Lord Tex made us obey orders and hit only the primary target that day or we would have been court-martialed and probably would have been shot.
Photo courtesy of the National Archives.

MARCH 4, 1945

Mission #30

Destination: Ulm

Target: Ordnance Depot

At 0400 the orderly woke me with his usual, "Mission today, Sir, breakfast at 0430, briefing at 0530."

"About time," I muttered. I didn't take long to get to the mess hall. I was anxious to get rolling again. This would be my thirtieth mission. Only five more after this one. I paused for a passing minute and thought of the other boys who hadn't returned. I wondered if they felt the same as I with only a few more to go? Better get my thoughts in order. Each mission could be the last.

"The target for today, gentlemen, is an ordnance depot at Ulm, Germany. Our boys on the ground are giving Jerry hell and our job is to make sure Jerry doesn't have the munitions to fight back," our commander said. "Also, and listen up: If any of you guys have a chance to bomb the bridge over the Rhine River near Remagen, Don't! I repeat, Don't! Our ground troop boys are getting real close to taking it and Patton wants to run his tanks across it and then keep it open for supplies."

I slowly turned to Tex and said, "Damn, if we had taken that bridge out, Patton would've had us shot for disobeying orders."

Tex looked my way and said, "Obey orders first and foremost, I keep telling you Eddie," while giving me one of his wisecrack smiles.

I didn't mind this time; I deserved the sarcasm. We could've been shot!

Our mission was uneventful. We only saw a few bursts of flak and all ships returned safely. One thing more the mission did do, besides getting me closer to home; this was the fourteenth consecutive day the Eighth Air Force flew bombing raids, a new record for the Eighth. It seems our weather here at Molesworth was worse than at other fields. I was happy to be finished and for not seeing much flak. The thought of taking out Remagen Bridge and then having to face our CO, Lt. Col. Richard Cole, was bad enough.

Here we are taxiing into position for our mission to Ulm.
Photo courtesy of the National Archives.

Oxygen masks were usually ordered on at altitudes of 10,000 feet. At altitudes necessary for bombing (20,000 feet or more), if we had not worn gloves and heated suits, frostbite would occur within seconds. Many of us learned to live with it. Photo courtesy of the National Archives.

MARCH 7, 1945

Mission #31

Destination: Dortmund-Harpenerweg

Target: Synthetic Oil Refinery

Again today, I was assigned to another plane, Lieutenant McClurg on the ship, *Lucille*. We had 10/10 cloud cover with tops at ten thousand feet. *Beautiful flying up here above the clouds*, I thought to myself.

"Flak ahead, boys, looks like Jerry has found the range on the boys up front, get your flak suits on," the pilot said. He didn't have to tell me; I had seen the bursts from our bubble.

It looked pretty thick. The flak was all around us. I could see some ships taking hits. *My God*, I thought, *not this close to finishing my tour*. After bombs away I watched closely, trying to see if they were on target. I was pressing up against the Plexiglas when I glanced up to see a ship out front take a direct hit.

"Lead ship, high squadron, just took a hit in the nose!" the co-pilot shouted. "Damn, a guy is falling out!"

I thought of Tex and Haynes immediately. Haynes was piloting his own ship today while Tex was flying co-pilot with Lt. Owen Knutzen's crew.

"Anyone know what plane that is?" I asked. Not hearing any answer, I watched closely the guy who was sailing towards us. It was as if he were falling in slow motion.

"He doesn't have a chute!" the bombardier yelled. "He's coming too close! Oh my God we're going to hit him!"

Within a second this boy was swept under our nose. As he passed, our eyes met.

"Oh my Lord," I said quietly, "I know that fellow. He's only been here a few days. This was his third mission."

I made my way back to my seat and wondered what it must have been like for him, the terror he must have been going through. What a way to get it. Falling thousands of feet with no chute and no chance of surviving. *Maybe he'll pass out before he hits.*

"Everyone, got your chutes on?" asked the pilot. "Check in."

We all checked in. I heard the ball turret gunner remind him that there was not enough room down there for a chute but did have his safety harness on.

Not much was said after that. We made our turn with the group and were heading home. The flak was disappearing and we didn't see many enemy fighters. We had seventy-four P-51s along for insurance. Enemy fighters were one thing, but that damned flak! Well, there wasn't much we could do about that stuff. So we hoped for the best and for a little luck.

Within a few minutes I heard one of our gunners say, "Bandit at two o'clock. He's closing fast."

I grabbed my weapon and swung around to get a shot. But by the time I was ready to fire, this thing flashed by us. "What the hell was that?" the pilot asked.

Jesus Christ, I thought, that's gotta be one of those new jets the Jerrys are developing. It was so damn fast I couldn't get off a shot.

"Sir, I think its one of those new Komets, jet fighters—or some faster than hell thing the Krauts have invented," someone answered. "Boy, she sure was fast."

We better get this war over with in a hurry or start making our own jet fighters. How can we hit something that moves that fast?

After landing, I saw Tex and Haynes at de-briefing. They had both seen the lead plane blow up but they didn't know the boy who was blown out without a chute.

Tex then said, "Eddie, let me buy you a beer."

"Sure thing," I answered, "let me turn in my report."

"Any word on those jet fighters we saw today sir?" I asked the de-briefing officer.

"Not too much Lieutenant, I mean, we know how fast they fly, and that their flight time is only a few minutes because most of their fuel is consumed on ascent. Why? They didn't bother you, did they?" he asked.

"No, sir. Nothing but...aw, just forget it."

And with that, I was well on my way to forgetting the entire mission. *Nothing I can do about it now.* And as far as a fellow being blown out of a ship, well sometimes you just have to think, "thank the Lord it wasn't me," and be on your way. If you think too much about this stuff you'll end up on a funny farm for sure.

We headed over to the officers' club for a couple of drinks and a look-see at the wall map tracking the progress of our ground forces, but I was really too tired to pay much attention, so I just finished my beer and smoke and headed to my barracks for a little rest.

This is the ball turret gunner's position, Sergeant Vowels' domain. No room for a parachute in here. These guys were closed and locked in position with their chest nearly hitting their knees. Vowels was one heck of a gunner and really knew his business but I wouldn't change jobs with him for anything, especially since some men died when they became stuck and the plane was forced to make a wheels-up belly landing. What a horrible way to die. Thank God I was nearly six feet tall, too tall for the ball turret. Photo courtesy of the National Archives.

This is a German jet, a Messerschmitt 262, prior to being shot down by one of our escorts just as he was about to shoot down one of our P-51 Mustangs. Photo courtesy of the National Archives.

This is a captured Messerschmitt 262 Jet. The German pilot flew it to a friendly field and surrendered. Photo courtesy of the National Archives.

PART THREE

THE END IS NEAR

In the next five days we flew three missions. A benzol plant at Essen, a marshalling yard at Schwerte, and a railway center at Betzdorf. Our missions by now almost seemed routine, although I was still going through the churning stomachs and frayed nerves, wondering if my luck would hold out.

These were my thirty-second, thirty-third, and thirty-fourth missions. Only one more and my tour would be finished. One more and I would get to go home. The mission to Schwerte was in the ship *Old Black Magic*, and my mission to Betzdorf was in the ship *Redwing*.

The weather was getting better with the passing season and the flying less threatening except for those damn German jets. I swear, if the Germans had brought them to the air battle sooner and had been able to keep them in the air longer, we'd have been in one hell of a mess.

MARCH 20, 1945

Mission #35

Destination: Zossen

Target: German Headquarters

Your target for today, gentlemen, will be the German High Command Headquarters at Zossen." What a way to finish my tour! We would be hitting the Hun at the control center of this great world war. Our payload will be five-hundred-pound incendiary bombs. We would burn the bastards out, as they had done to countless others.

By the time of my long-awaited final mission, General Bradley had taken the Remagen Bridge and General Patton was advancing across it. Boy, was I glad that Tex had followed orders on that March fourth raid. I still get nervous when I think about my almost great error of judgment.

Before we arrived at the target we were cut off the bomb run by some B-24s from another bomb group coming in from the north. We had to go around on a second run. Going around again on a bomb run could be suicide. I saw the bombardier cross his fingers.

"Sir, some jet aircraft are south of the target but seem to be holding there and not attacking," the radio operator said.

"Good, keep me informed," the pilot answered.

Thank goodness for that, I thought. We had eighty-two of our little friends beside, above and below us; I hoped they could take care of the Kraut jets if need be.

I had heard too many stories about men flying their final missions. They were uncanny, these stories; so many men killed their last time out. I was on double-alert and wary.

I was flying with Lieutenant Richeson. None of my original crew was in the air. We were also right behind the lead ship. Not a good position to be in. Well, was any position good for that matter? All bad omens.

Eight hours and thirty minutes after takeoff, after a long and nervous mission, we landed at Molesworth. Upon landing I sat at my navigator's table for a few minutes. What do I do now? Should I think about staying on, volunteering for more missions, or consider a transfer to the Pacific? What about going home, Betty June, marriage? I'd better think about it for a while and decide later. Right now I was just happy to be finished.

After de-briefing I was met by Haynes, Tex and Donovan; my comrades-in-arms for many months and the best friends any fellow could ever have. After a pat on the back from each, we headed over to the officers' club for a couple dozen rounds. Yes, I thought, best to wait and decide later.

Recently, I had received two letters from Betty June that didn't make any sense. She wrote that she was unsure about getting married but I did not know why. We had dated all through high school and now, when I was almost ready to come home, this. I just assumed, you know, if I got through my thirty-five missions, I would return and marry the only sweetheart I ever had.

March 22, 1945

Darling,

I have received your last letters but I do not understand. We can talk when I get back.

I have finished my tour here, and could come home, but I am staying here. I want to see this war end.

It's nearly spring now and the flying weather is grand. Here's a picture we took in front of the hut. I will take some more if possible.

When you finally decide about getting married then I'll stop fighting. Until then, I'll try to help end this war, or go down trying.

I Love You,
Edward

Ten days had passed and I was bored nearly to death. Paperwork was not for me. I decided to fly on another mission.

On March 28, I volunteered to fly a mission to the Branden-Burgische Motorenwerke near Berlin. I was to replace an ill navigator on Lieutenant Fredrickson's crew of the 427th Bomb Squadron, aboard the ship, *Jigger Roache II*.

The night before the mission, I was told that the navigator; Art Herman was feeling well enough to fly, so I was ordered at the last minute to wait for the next mission.

By the end of the day, I learned that Fredrickson's plane failed to assemble and bombed with another group over Hanover.

After dinner with some of the boys I decided to write home.

March, 29, 1945

Dear Mother,

The old man said that you were watching each taxi that stopped near the house in hopes that I would be the party in it. Well, that's why I hesitate to say I am coming home. Seems something always happens when you count too much on one thing. Well, in about three weeks you can start watching then. I'd say three weeks after you get this letter I'll be knocking on the front door. But not until then.

I hope Bobby is doing OK in his subjects at school. It means a lot if he is to take part in sports. He may be in the Army soon so lessons are important unless he wants to spend his years scrubbing floors.

Love to all,
Edward

MARCH 30, 1945

Mission #36

Destination: Bremen

Target: Submarine Yards

Strange as it must seem to some, I was glad to be back in the thick of things, even though Bremen was still a dangerous place to linger for long. This was my first mission to the submarine yards, but not the Eighth's.

I had heard stories of the Bloody 100th's mission in the skies over Bremen in October, 1943, when they lost seven planes and seventy men.[9]

By this point the skies were less filled with enemy fighters. We had taken care of most of the oil depots. The Germans had fine pilots and good planes but lacked the fuel to put them up except in regions that they felt they had to defend, such as Berlin. The air war had made shambles of their rail systems, oil depots, cities and morale.

I was once again flying with Haynes who had been promoted from co-pilot to pilot. His ship, the *Duchess' Granddaughter*, was positioned one ship behind the squadron lead, which was piloted by Captain Cunningham. Tex was assigned as Cunningham's co-pilot for this mission. It was good to be back in familiar company. I felt somewhat safe.

We were greeted at the target by heavy flak. The group's lead plane was hit immediately and began to fade to the rear of the formation. Nobody knew if they crash-landed, bailed out, or made it back.

We had learned the fate of the *Jigger Roache II* from the mission two days earlier. The pilot had managed to make a wheels-up crash landing in Poland. The co-pilot was killed and the navigator I was to replace, was wounded. We weren't sure when they would be returning to England. Lucky again for me, I guess.

---

[9] Jablonski, *Flying Fortress*, 195

These are contrails while on a raid over Bremen. Missions were bad enough without telegraphing where we were headed. Many enemy fighters would sneak up behind us using these contrails as cover and try to blast us out of the sky. Photo courtesy of the National Archives.

When we touched down at Molesworth, I had made my decision. This would be my final time. The war was coming to an end and I had done my share. Too many close calls. I knew my luck was running out. It had to be.

I had a long talk with Haynes and Tex at the officers' club. Haynes wanted to continue piloting his own plane for a few more missions. Tex had completed his thirty-second mission and had but three to go. They both would be in the air for a couple more weeks anyway. But me, well, it was time to let someone else have a turn.

I soon made up my mind to transfer to the Pacific and fly those giant bombers, the B-29s. An old friend of mine from home, George Hughes, (who had played football for our cross-town rivals), was over there doing his part as a gunner. I didn't want him to have all the fun.

I told Tex and Haynes I had to write Blue Jay and let her know that I was done here and of my intentions.

March 30, 1945

My Darling,

I've stopped flying now and I'm coming home. I figure my luck is just about all gone, because I had a few close calls a while back, near the end of the game. I figured I'd better be getting home if I ever were to get there. So I stopped flying.

I guess I'll be flying soon again, though, because I'm going to volunteer for the Pacific after I'm home for twenty-one days. That will be fine flying there, because I'll be in a faster, and much more comfortable ship, more dangerous too, I guess, but it's fun.

You know, Darling, through the war you see a lot of funny things happen. You wonder why they happen. You face a lot of things you thought you could never face, but when you are through facing such things, you look back and say "nothing to it." I believe I can sweat out the Pacific and get back. I never thought I'd finish here but I did. So I'll get by there too.

I've had enough of B-17s. It's the best heavy bomber we have, though Jerry can shoot the hell out of it, but it still brings us home. The old lady can take a lot.

I can't tell you anything about the base or the missions except that I'm through with them.

As for England, someday I'll tell you all about it and maybe show it to you. England is OK but I love my own country too much, and my own state and the city of Norfolk. I can't change just because another place is cleaner or larger or smaller, etc.

I hope your work in school is coming along okay and that you take good care of yourself.

No matter how long we wait for each other, no matter how long, remember this. I love you and someday I'll come to take you home, maybe a month, a year, ten years, but love me and for God sake wait for me with patience. I live to live with you.

All my love always,
Edward

END OF THE LINE

My time here was at last over except for mustering out and waiting for a transfer to the Pacific theater. I was ready for whatever came next. These B-17s were great machines. These battered ladies would bring us back alive time and time again when most other aircraft would have folded up and gone in. However, the newer B-29s were much bigger, faster and more comfortable to fly in because of the pressurized, heated cabins. I couldn't wait to be part of a new crew and to be airborne again in one of those babies.

My last mission was on March 30, 1945. Since then I spent much of my time doing follow-up paper work and mess like that. On April 15, I had the occasion to be questioned, along with Tex, by one of the newly assigned paper-pusher officers concerning why we wanted to go to the Pacific. Tex, though, had a couple more missions to chalk up.

During the conversation, this guy asked Tex, "Now let's see, Lieutenant, your record says you have three years of schooling. What college did you attend?"

Tex, looking a little embarrassed, hesitated.

"What college, Lieutenant?" he was asked again.

"Well sir..." Tex began, "I didn't go to college."

The officer answered, "It says here three years of schooling. Is that false?"

"No, sir," Tex answered with his eyes welling up with water. "You see sir, it was three years...total schooling."

"What do you mean by that, Lieutenant?" the officer said, raising his voice.

"I only made it through the third grade, sir. You see, I had to quit school to work and help feed my family."

This officer was silent for a few seconds and then said abruptly, "You only made it through the third damn grade? You gotta be kidding me. Why in the hell are you piloting a B-17? We're sending men up with a guy who has a third-grade education—Jesus!"

I looked this officer squarely in the eye. "Is that all you have to say to this man? After all he's done? After all he's been through, while you sit here on your fat ass away from the fighting, doing nothing but pushing papers? "

He looked surprised and, feeling my anger, quickly said, "That's all, gentlemen, you are both excused."

I slowly half-way saluted, turned and said, "Yes, sir," then exited saying to Tex, "That sorry-ass-son-of-bitch. I should go back in there and kick the hell out of him for treating you like that."

Tex knew my ways and quickly said, "Forget it, Eddie, that bastard wouldn't know how to board a B-17, much less fight in one. Besides, you just did kick the hell out of him."

The very next day Tex was leading the entire Eighth Air Force on a bombing raid to destroy a railroad bridge in Straubing, Germany. He was the lead flight and the lead pilot! Don't know how ol' Tex managed that with only a third-grade education!

This is a picture of "Hell's Angels" returning to Molesworth
after a mission. What a sight to see.
Photo courtesy of the National Archives.

This is the lead crew on a raid to Hamburg, Germany on March 20, 1945.
The pilot is Capt. William E. Eisenhart, back row extreme right.
My friend and a great pilot, flying as co-pilot on this mission is
Alfred M. (Tex) Holmes pictured here to the left of Eisenhart.
Photo courtesy of the National Archives.

LEAVING MOLESWORTH

Looking back and thinking of my thirty-six missions over Germany, and realizing that I had played but a small part, brought to mind the many heroes who took part in liberating Europe.

Even though I didn't know all the men who flew in "Hell's Angels" and the 303rd, I knew their stories, told and retold by others.

One of those stories belongs to Lt. Jack Mathis and his brother Mark. Jack Mathis was on a mission to Vegesack as bombardier on the lead ship, *The Duchess*. As trained, the other planes in a group would commence bombing on his release using the bombsight, which was connected to the autopilot. While on the bomb run no evasive action is taken until the bombs are dropped and the pilot regains control of the plane.

Just before Mathis was to drop his bombs his ship was hit by flak in the nose, nearly taking off his arm and wounding him in the abdomen. The force of the flak burst threw him and the navigator against the plane's bulkhead, nearly ten feet away. Mathis, knowing the whole group was bombing on his release, crawled back to his bombsight and released his bombs exactly over the target. As always, the rest of the squadron followed his lead. Mathis reached over to close the bomb bay doors and once that final task was completed, he fell over his bombsight and died. Jack Mathis received the Medal of Honor for his heroism.

After learning of his brother's death, Mark, who had been flying in medium bombers, asked to transfer to his brother's squadron. Mark wanted to finish his brother's tour. Jack had flown only fourteen missions before his death. It was Mark's fourth mission on the same plane, *The Duchess*. It was on a raid to bomb the shipyard at Kiel, Germany that this good ship and its crew was reported missing, and never to be heard from again.[10]

There are other heroes such as radio operator T/Sgt Forrest Vosler, also of the 303rd. After being wounded in his legs, chest,

---

[10] Freeman, 27, 28, 267; Jablonski, 118, 120

face and eyes, Vosler was able to continue fighting, though nearly blind. By touch alone, he reassembled his radio and made contact again. His plane, *Jersey Bounce Jr.*, had to ditch. Vosler made it to the wing and was able to keep hold of a badly wounded crewmember until others could get them into one of the dinghies. He spent ten months in the hospital recovering from his wounds. Sergeant Vosler also received the Medal of Honor.[11]

We remember these boys and many others in various groups of the Eighth Air Force, such as Maynard Smith of the 306th Bomber Group, Walter Truemper and a crew member, Archibald Mathies of the 351st Bomber Group and Robert Femoyer of the 447th Bomber Group. These brave men did their duty and put their lives on the line for their country. Each was awarded, posthumously, the Medal of Honor, except for Smith who miraculously survived.[12]

Maynard Smith on his first mission, exited his ball turret position when it ceased to rotate and saw the radio operator and the two waist gunners putting on their parachutes, getting ready to jump. With a fire in the radio room Smith could not see if the pilots had jumped. Since the ship was still flying straight and level he decided to stay on board and fight the fire with the extinguishers. The plane did stay in formation, meaning the pilots were still aboard, alive and in control. Smith had also noticed a fire in the rear of the plane and started to put it out when he saw the bloody, badly wounded tail gunner. After giving his crewmember first aid, Smith returned to fight what was by now a raging fire. After using all the extinguishers available he used the only option he had left...he urinated on the rest. As ammunition boxes started to explode he tossed some of them out of the plane and moved the others away from the remaining fire. Smith fought the flames, continued to look after the tail gunner and shot at enemy fighters from the two waist gun positions. The plane was beaten up pretty bad but made it back to base. Thanks to Smith, the remaining crew lived to tell the tale, and to fight another day. I don't know why he decided to stay with the plane. I'm not sure he knew. I remember my first mission and how nervous I was when I saw our lead plane blown out of the sky. You can bet your last nickel on this; If I had seen my fellow crew

[11] Freeman, *The Mighty Eighth*, 102, 269
[12] ibid, 267

members getting ready to bail out, I would've jumped, and in a flash! Smith flew only four more missions before being reassigned to a ground job. It seemed being labeled the first living Medal of Honor recipient in the Eighth Air Force had an adverse effect on him and he became difficult to handle. Many men are troublesome when it comes to taking and following orders. Many men are great fighters. Smith, as it turned out, was both.[13]

Navigator Walter Truemper, along with ball turret gunner Archibald Mathies, made their way to the cockpit after a shell exploded, killing the co-pilot and wounding the pilot. The bombardier, thinking the aircraft would not make it, ordered the crew to bail out, then jumped himself. Truemper and Mathies removed the dead co-pilot's badly mangled body while maintaining control of the aircraft using only the ailerons and elevators. Mathies, who had some limited flying experience, took the wheel. With the glass blown out and gale force freezing wind gushing into the cockpit, both men took turns flying the ship back to their base at Polebrook. Once over the base the rest of the crew bailed out but Mathies and Truemper refused to abandon the unconscious pilot, electing instead to try and land the plane themselves. These two fellows made two passes at the runway, both too high. On their third try the plane stalled, then crashed, killing them both. The pilot survived the crash but died soon thereafter because of his wounds.[14]

Navigator Robert Femoyer, while on a raid to Merseberg was badly wounded in the back and side from flak but refused medical treatment and an injection of morphine, in order to keep his head clear and navigate the ship around known ground flak batteries. Crew members had to keep him propped up so he could see his maps and equipment because he was too week from loss of blood to sit down at his table. Only when his ship and crew were in safe air space did he allow the others to give him a shot of morphine, easing the pain from his wounds. Femoyer died shortly after landing.[15]

There were other amazing stories. Waist gunner Bob Sorenson was blown out of his plane without a chute. After watching his ship blow up before his eyes and falling thousands of feet, Sorenson was able to grab a passing parachute that was also blown from the plane.

[13] ibid, 30, 31, 267
[14] ibid, 108, 269, 270
[15] ibid, 180, 270, 271

He was able to attach it to his harness and made an unbelievable safe return.

Then there were men like Buck Dunn, who was from my old neighborhood of Ocean View, though I never knew him. Buck Dunn flew an incredible 104 missions! He was assigned to the 569th Bomb Squadron of the 390th Bomb Group. His 104 missions included nine to Berlin. He flew as a top turret gunner, a tail gunner and as a bombardier/nose gunner—104 missions![16]

There were the incomparable men who flew in my original crew, such as Alfred "Tex" Holmes, who saved us more than once. The time he put the plane into a backwards stall to put out a flaming engine, or the times he brought us back all shot up, saving us from sure death, were remarkable. Tex finished his tour with forty-two missions.

Eugene Haynes, our co-pilot, got his own plane and flew thirty-six missions. Ed Bartkowski flew twenty-three missions with Tex and was shot down on his twenty-fourth mission, the only mission he flew with another crew. Ed became a prisoner of war. The rest of our original crew, Tom Donovan (twenty-nine missions), Wendell Sprague Jr. (thirty-one missions), Dennis Hejna (thirty-six missions), Joe Prehatny (thirty-one missions), and Don Vowels (thirty-five missions) were all exceptionally brave men.

All of these fellows and thousands more just like them did their duty, receiving neither recognition nor reward. These guys were the faceless, unsung heroes, every damn one of them.

And I know for a fact that any of them, if asked if they thought of themselves as heroes, would say, "Hell no. I'm no hero. The real heroes are the boys who are still there, buried all over Europe."

"Their families are steadfast heroes for their silent sacrifice of their fathers, brothers and sons to free from the arms of hell itself, all the freedom-loving people of Europe. They are the real heroes. Not me, I just did the job that I was asked to do. I was damn glad to do it. And I would do it again."

The Eighth and Fifteenth Air Force, both fighting in the European Theater of Operations, lost thousands of aircraft and over 93,000 men. Of those, over 43,000 were killed or wounded and over

---

[16] ibid, 223

50,000 were captured or reported missing. Many, to this day, are still unaccounted for.

England, Europe and America, should never forget them.

You can be sure of one thing. I will never forget a single one of these brave, young men.

EPILOGUE

By Bill Albertson

After the war ended and my father returned home, he, like many soldiers, airmen, marines and sailors, had a tough time adjusting. His longtime sweetheart, Betty June, decided not to marry him. Apparently everything was still moving pretty fast and my father did not want to wait, and married someone else. After losing many friends in battle and having many, many close calls himself, I'm sure he didn't want to be alone any longer. It seems the letter his father sent him stating that war veterans would change, not the people back home, was correct. That marriage however, lasted only a short while. Once he learned how to re-connect to normal civilian life, things got a lot better for him.

Betty June and my father finally did marry on July 7, 1949. They settled in Norfolk, and moved into one of the houses his mother and father built on the lower Chesapeake Bay.

My mother and father had four children, two girls and two boys. The eldest daughter, their firstborn, Betty Kent, died of leukemia at four years of age, causing them great heartbreak while also proving to each other their enduring love.

On March 27, 1995 my father died. My mother died fourteen months later on May 31, 1996. They are buried in the family plot at Forest Lawn Cemetery in Norfolk, next to my sister and grandparents, his mother and father.

My hope in recounting this, my father's story, is so that all generations to come will realize the gallant efforts made by all families during that time in history…and to not forget their sacrifices.

A quote from one of our past presidents, John F. Kennedy, says it best:

"Let the word go forth from this time and place, to friend and foe alike, that the torch has been passed to a new generation of Americans—born in this century, tempered by war, disciplined by a hard and bitter peace, proud of our ancient heritage—and unwilling to witness or permit the slow undoing of those human rights to which this nation has always been committed, and to which we are committed today at home and around the world.

Let every nation know, whether it wishes us well or ill, that we shall pay any price, bear any burden, meet any hardship, support any friend, oppose any foe, to assure the survival and the success of liberty."

Ground crews like these good fellows kept us flying. Many a night they worked straight through to early morning, and later would wait and watch for their crews to return during the day. It was just as hard to these boys when their friends didn't return. We spent many hours in their tent drinking coffee, waiting for the call to head out.
Photo courtesy of the National Archives.

This is a flak helmet like the ones some of us wore. I don't know if this guy made it or not. Photo courtesy of the National Archives.

Enemy aircraft or enemy flak could and did do massive damage to our ships. A number of planes made it back but not all of the crewmembers who flew on them were so lucky. Photo courtesy of the National Archives.

This is a good picture after bombs away. This was the most dangerous time on a mission because the plane was on autopilot and could take no evasive action. At the bottom of this picture you can see the target going up in smoke. Photo courtesy of the National Archives.

Me and my co-pilot, Haynes. He's from New Mexico.
Tall, lanky, intelligent and a very good pilot. He's married, one child two
years old. This is his car. He has ears like an elephant.
He's a good boy. *Author's collection.*

Tom, from Boston, our lead bombardier. Tex, from Fort Worth, our first
pilot, now flying lead. Both are hot rocks, good boys. *Author's collection.*

Tex in the Astrodome. My peek hole. *Author's collection.*

Haynes in the left seat. Tex's territory. *Author's collection.*

This ship is named *Duchess' Daughter.* *Author's collection.*

Another of the "Iron Birds." *Author's collection.*

You've seen this ship's picture in *Life*. The old *Queen of Hearts*.
Author's collection.

Ed, the crew chief, keeps us flying. *Author's collection.*

"Tennessee," ground crew member of the ship. *Author's collection.*

Here's a picture we took in front of the hut. I will take more if possible.
Author's collection.

This is my older brother Douglas. He was a tough boy. He joked after the war about his stay in the hospital after being wounded by a Jap grenade and contracting malaria. He said he spent more time in the hospital than I did on my whole tour of thirty-six missions. Doug enlisted in the Marine Corps in December 1941 and made nine major landings from Guadalcanal through Okinawa, serving as a scout sniper in the First Marine Division. He was decorated for bravery and was awarded the Purple Heart.

Author's collection.

This is a picture of my father, Cyrus Kent Albertson, taken
while serving in France in WWI. *Author's collection.*

This is a picture of my father and his company. He is at the extreme left.
Author's collection.

HEADQUARTERS EIGHTH CORPS AREA
OFFICE OF THE AIR OFFICER

FORT SAM HOUSTON, TEXAS.
September 14,1925.

C. K. Albertson,
Packard Automobiles,
Norfolk, Va.

Dear Sir:-

Thank you very much for your letter of September 6th.

Feeling as I do that this is the most vital and important problem before our Nation today, it is indeed a pleasure to receive an expression of this nature, and truly encouraging in that it is representative, I believe, of what America feels on this subject.

Yours very truly,

Wm. Mitchell,
Colonel,A.S.

This is the actual letter to my father from
Col. William (Billy) Mitchell. *Author's collection.*

This is our football team of 1942, Granby High School.
By the way, we won that Thanksgiving Day game, but missed the state
championship because of our tie on October 11.
There were some tough boys on that team.
Author's collection.

1942　FOOT

First Row: Ray Swigart, Red White, Edward Rhodes, Reid Spencer, Doug Whitehurst, Bill Vaeth, Hal
Second Row: Bus Wigmore, Tim Vogt, Bobby Baxter, Forest Hill, Stanworth Brinkley, Braxton Harrell,
Third Row: Warren Parr, Dick White, Hal Ware, Bernard Chitty, John Stell, Winston Williamson,
Fourth Row: Coach Story, Ray Emanuelson, George Lilly, Billy Breeden, Richard Brinkley, Obie

FOOTBALL LETTERMEN

Al Nowitzky	Jimmy Head	Bernard Chitty
Martin Whitehurst	Buck Harris	B. G. Harrell
Obie Whitehurst	Carlton Seay	Winston Williamson
Doug Whitehurst	Bud Chandler	Anton Wrzesinski
Richard Brinkley	Artie Shaw	Reid Spencer
Easy Rhodes	Claiborne Fitchett	Ray Swiggart
Hal Ware	Eddie Albertson	BillVaeth
Red White	Eddie Guy	Dick White
Gene Eskey	Stanworth Brinkley	Hal Mapes

BALL TEAM

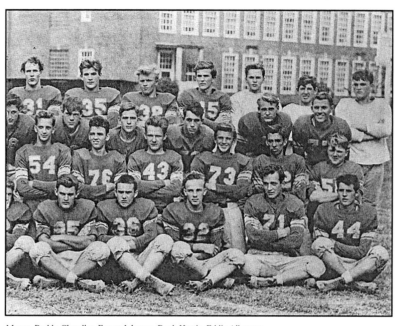

Mapes, Buddy Chandler, Ernest Johnson, Buck Harris, Eddie Albertson
Kilby Malbon, Claiborne Fitchett, Si Harland, Louis Peters, Blanco Wallin
Billy Laurence, Louis Akehurst, Artie Shaw, Anton Wrzesinski
Whitehurst, Jimmy Head, Gene Eskey, Martin Whitehurst, Edward Guy, Ronald McLean, Billy Harrison

FOOTBALL SCHEDULE

	Granby	Opponents
Sept. 20—Wilson, N.C.	18	0
Sept. 27—Crewe	45	18
Oct. 4—Jefferson, Sr.	7	2
Oct. 11—Thomas Jefferson	6	6
Oct. 17—Rocky Mount	20	6
Oct. 31—Hampton	34	8
Nov. 8—Newport News	33	0
Nov 14—Maury	20	0
Nov. 20—Wilson	7	2

And this, my friends, is Betty June.
My high school sweetheart and later my wife.
If there was an angel on earth, she was truly one.
Author's collection.

About the Author

Bill Albertson's ancestors have fought in the American Revolution, the War of 1812, the Civil War and in World Wars I and II.

Mr. Albertson lives and works in Virginia Beach, Virginia, where for over thirty years he has been active in the real estate sale and investment business.

He continues to study and write about the brave men who served and fought for their country.

INDEX

1153965

Made in the USA